LEADING WITH YOUR IMAGINATION

A framework for Creative Leadership

SCOTT J WAKEFIELD

Published by Envision Books,

A division of Creative Synthesis Ltd.

Aurora, CO

ISBN: 978-0982485019, 978-0982485026

ISBN: 978-0982485033 (digital)

EDUCATION / Leadership
BUSINESS & ECONOMICS / Workplace Culture
SELF-HELP / Personal Growth / Success

Artwork by Scott J. Wakefield

Design by Tracey Tassinari, Joyage Studio

Printed in the United States of America

1st Edition

LEADING WITH YOUR IMAGINATION

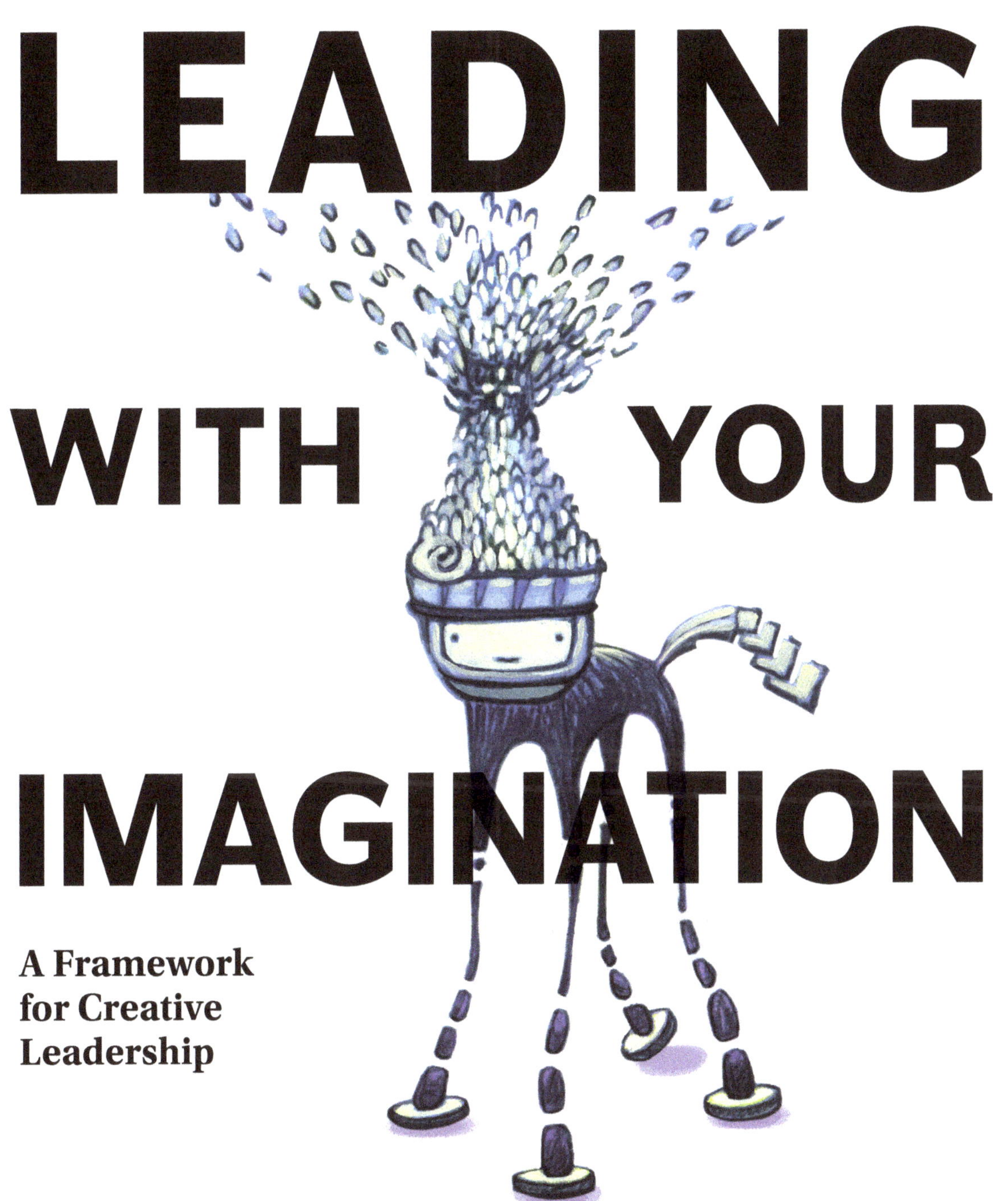

A Framework for Creative Leadership

CONTENTS

PREFACE:

I am an artist, illustrator, teacher, and academic leader. I am a husband and a father. Until recently, *I did not consider myself a writer.* When I first began to write, I had to google the difference between a "Preface" and a "Prologue." Here in the Preface, I want to give you a sense of who I am and how I came to write a book on *Creative Leadership.* To that end, I will briefly introduce myself, describe some aspects of my creative journey, and acknowledge the Source of all that is good in my life.

As a professional illustrator, I studied art at three different institutions and developed a successful art practice in children's books for the better part of my life. But when I go to the bookstore – I don't go to the art section or the picture book section. I usually find myself in one of two places: Self-help and Business.

Why self-help? Well, that's obvious to my friends and family. And the business section is where I find books about leadership!

A few years ago now, I discovered a book by Tom Rath called *Strengths-Finder 2.0.* His book suggested that I could approach my life and leadership from a strengths-based perspective. I liked this idea of *leading* with my strengths. So, I read the book and took the strengths assessment.

HERE ARE MY TOP STRENGTHS ACCORDING TO RATH:

1. **Belief:** guided by core values that are unchanging

2. **Futuristic:** inspired by the future and what could be, motivating others with visions of a better future

3. **Developer:** recognizes and cultivates the potential they see in others

4. **Responsibility:** takes ownership of what they say they will do, committed to stable values such as honesty and loyalty

5. **Significance:** desires to be very important in the lives of others, independent, seeks for meaning

Significance was not something I understood as a strength, so that was a new and important insight. Other than that, I was not really surprised by these results. My top five seemed to resonate with the truth of my personality, interests, talents, and core beliefs. In fact, just reading the brief summaries next to each strength will tell you much about who I am, what I believe, and what I value.

The choice to introduce myself with these five words should also tell you about the importance I place on words and ideas that convey meaning and truth. I have been inspired and fascinated by the power of words since I was a little boy.

At one point, after renovating our home, I organized the basement crawl space we were using as storage. I found a small notebook with a hard metal cover among my important keepsakes – it was my quote book! I remembered that it was one of the items I got from my great-grandfather's estate when I was about seven years old. He had left it to my maternal grandmother.

You might think that I would have filled it with doodles or drawings. However, by the time I entered high school, I had filled that little notebook with quotes – tiny treasures of wisdom – that I had written, or heard, and wanted to remember. That little quote book is an early indication of my persistent interest in words and ideas – a trait I must have inherited from my English-teacher father. But more than a collection of profound ideas, I have come to see the contents of that little book as a certain set of ideals that seem to have helped guide my decisions and character ever since.

At some point in high school, my girlfriend (who is now my wife) must have sensed the value that I placed on those quotes. She decided to type them up for me and I kept that version of the quote book in my important papers – papers that have traveled with me for more than 25 years. During the initial stages of writing this book, as I read the quotes again, I began to identify certain groupings or themes. So, I decided to categorize them based on the main idea of the quote.

In the nearly 150 quotes, I found large groupings in support of seven particular themes:

Theme #1: Be a Good Human: Forgive. Be sincere, unselfish, and kind. Don't gossip.

Theme #2: See People as People: Be a friend, see the good in others, smile, listen. Look beyond the outward appearance and embrace differences.

Theme #3: Develop Integrity and Good Character: Be humble, honest, modest. Manifest your beliefs in your actions, keep confidences, and be yourself. Truth will endure.

Theme #4: Aspire toward Greatness: Set high expectations, make a difference, and give it your best! Leave your mark, do it well, and don't be afraid to join the race.

Theme #5: Live with Optimism and Positivity: (This was the largest group!) Be happy, confident, enthusiastic, and hopeful. Don't succumb to fear or get bogged down with your troubles. Life is what you make it – make it great!

Theme #6: Work Hard: Make hay while the sun shines and make the most of today. Keep busy with good things, don't procrastinate, and don't waste time.

Theme #7: Take Responsibility: Get involved – don't wait to act or avoid difficulty; God helps those who help themselves – no excuses. This last theme contained the most humorous quote (at least to my young mind). It read, "Excuses are like belly buttons: Everybody has them and they're all useless now."

When I completed the work of organizing them into themes, I suddenly saw fascinating parallels between my identified strengths and the quotes I chose.

QUOTE THEME	RELATED STRENGTH	RELATED STRENGTH
Be a Good Human	*Belief* (guided by core values)	*Responsibility* (integrity)
See People as People	*Developer* (cultivate potential in others)	
Develop Integrity and Good Character	*Responsibility* (committed to honest, loyalty)	
Aspire Towards Greatness	*Significance* (seeking importance)	*Futuristic* (motivate others with positive visions)
Live with Optimism and Positivity	*Futuristic* (motivate others with positive visions)	*Belief* (guided by core values)
Work Hard	*Developer* (working toward potential)	*Responsibility*
Take Responsibility	*Responsibility*	

As you read this book and get to know me, you may see other connections between this list and the concepts we discuss. In contrast to Theme #6 (Work Hard) and Theme #7 (Take Responsibility), my favorite quote in the sixth grade was this: "Genius is the ability to avoid hard work!"

By this definition, I am not a genius. I have been working way too hard for that to be true. Freelancing as an illustrator, working full-time as an art educator, providing for a family of seven, and being committed to church service means I have spent long hours in the studio before the day job and after dinner. Putting in 60+-hour work weeks has been the norm. In spite of this reality, however, living and working at the intersection of art, teaching, and leadership has been extremely satisfying for me.

The alternative career path (routine, predictable, safe) was never a consideration. My wife and I often joked that if I wanted something predictable, I should have become a dentist. But I always knew I would be creating art. Perhaps I was seeking significance, but I also think I could see the potential of art to give meaning to our lives. Apparently, the allure of meaningful creation was more important to me than seeking financial security with less uncertainty.

Yes, I knew all about the starving artist stereotype. But even after choosing an art school and committing to this path, it never crossed my mind to research the average income of an illustrator. Why? I guess it didn't really matter. I saw my education as a high-risk investment with the possibility of exponential returns (and that's my futuristic strength showing through...).

When I attended my grandmother's 90th birthday I looked around the large gymnasium where her eight children and 40+ grandchildren (and great grandchildren) had gathered. I noticed an interesting commonality – more than half of the group were teachers of some kind. A little less than half were in the medical professions, and then there was a small group of tech/business entrepreneurs. That was just my mom's side; there are many teachers in my Dad's family as well. Teaching is in my blood.

Even while pursuing my first degree in art, I knew that I wanted to become a teacher; in part because I had been powerfully influenced by good teachers my entire life. In particular, my middle-grade art teacher who made art fun, and my high school teachers who pushed me beyond whatever natural talent I had. Moving into higher education, I spent nine years getting a master's degree in Studio Art (yes, do that math!?), and another decade of teaching at the college level. I am a witness to and a product of the immeasurable influence of good teaching.

Leadership has been a part of my life since high school, perhaps before. As a youth, I earned my Eagle Scout award, participated in student government, and held leadership positions in my congregation. I believe in the potential of leadership to change the world in positive ways, and I have always strived to lead with integrity, optimism, and creativity.

Some might see art, teaching, and leadership as three separate and distinct disciplines; but for me, they are all connected. Together, they have become a comprehensive approach to thinking, working, and leading that inspires growth and innovation. I call this strategy: *Creative Leadership.*

HINGE POINTS

I didn't expect art and teaching to merge with leadership in this way, but now that they have, it makes perfect sense. Looking back at significant moments or turning points in my creative career, I can see the strands of connections that have led me to this point.

"That would be really hard."
Some time in my first years at college, I told my Grandpa what I was thinking of doing with my art. We were driving near Palisades Reservoir on some curvy mountain roads and I was in the back seat (holding

on to both door handles to keep my balance). I wasn't *exactly* sure what it would look like, but I explained that I wanted to "make illustrations that would teach principles of leadership." I am also not sure of his exact words, but in essence, he said, "That would be really hard." His realism bumped right up against my idealistic optimism. I knew he was right – but my response was, "I'm gonna do it!" I have never forgotten that moment. Perhaps it has been providing me with motivation for many years, but I never imagined writing a book to make it happen.

"You have to get the vision."
Before I started college, I served as a full-time missionary for the Church of Jesus Christ of Latter-day Saints. I spent two years in the northern half of Portugal. I developed proficiency in Portuguese and taught people about Jesus Christ and His church on the earth today. The mission had around 200 missionaries and was led by a mission president. My mission president, Joseph West, taught me an important concept. He explained that since we were doing the Lord's work, we needed to know what the Lord envisioned for our part of the work. He described a process of humbling ourselves, preparing for success, asking, seeking, and coming to understand the Lord's will (the vision) for ourselves, our groups, and the work in our area. In many of our training sessions he said, "You have to get the vision." This idea of having God give me an indication of what He wanted from me became a powerful spiritual concept that I have tried to implement ever since. Through that intention, I have come to know that working toward a vision is also an integral part of creative leadership.

"You're not creative enough to teach creativity in a creative way."
My undergrad degree at Art Center College of Art and Design was highly focused on the technical and conceptual aspects of Illustration. It

was a great education. But when I decided to get a master's degree I was more interested in the process or the thinking behind making art. I wanted to study and teach creativity. I wrote a graduate paper on the subject and developed what I called the "Components of the Creative Process." I proposed a number of thesis ideas to my advisor, including a heavily researched presentation to teach ideas about creativity. After reviewing my proposal, the sentiment he communicated with me was, "You're not creative enough to teach creativity in a creative way." He also told me that it was morally irresponsible to teach people to be illustrators and that doing a children's book was not really graduate-level work. So... yeah...

His attitudes actually helped to inform my belief about creativity, as all-encompassing and inclusive – not limited to a particular domain, method, or group. And apparently, my vision of completing my master's degree was stronger than his negativity. In the end, I developed an acceptable (to me and him) and highly successful thesis project that led to completing my degree, self-publishing a picture book, creating a marketable style, and boosting my career in children's books. But I never forgot my desire to study and teach creativity.

"Creativity and Visual Thinking"
Shortly after I was hired as the Chair of Art & Design at the Community College of Aurora, I noticed the title of a class in the system catalog. It was called "MGD 106 Creativity and Visual Thinking." As we redesigned the foundation level courses that every student would need to take, I made sure this was part of the core. They needed to know about the components of the creative process! This was also my chance to teach creativity, creatively – and I took it! I created a course where students engaged in design challenges, used playing cards to create

sculptural interpretations of abstract concepts, made music together with random household objects, explored systems thinking by playing games, built newspaper bridges to understand design, and then constructed a large walkable labyrinth at the end of each semester.

I imagine that each of us could make a similar list of hinge points or moments of decision that have influenced our path. These are just a few of literally millions of ordinary moments and decisions that have helped me to this point.

A NOTE ABOUT FAITH

There is one element in my life that, *more than anything else,* has influenced my path, my ways of thinking, and my understanding of creativity. And that is my faith in God as The Great Creator. It doesn't seem right to try to explain the components of the creative process or principles of creative leadership without acknowledging the Source of all truth, creativity, intelligence, and leadership. I believe that all principles of creativity and leadership are inspired by His nature and the laws of the universe.

Some of you are squirming right now. That's okay. You don't have to understand or share my belief in God to embrace creative leadership. You don't have to be religious or spiritual to apply the ideas in this book. But if you are religious, or spiritual, or choose to humbly consider my deeply-held beliefs, this brief description of spiritual truths may give you a deeper appreciation for the principles taught in this book.

You will find my references to faith or religious leaders, if included at all, are limited. I'll explain it here so that it is not obtrusive. I see God as a Father, who knows and loves each of us. We are his children – first as intelligent spirit children in a premortal realm – then as a human soul with both body and spirit – and finally as a perfected being, similar in nature to our Heavenly Parents. Because of our divine parentage, we have divine characteristics and inherent creative potential. Our innate creativity and imagination are unique spiritual gifts. In addition, He has granted us agency (the ability to act instead of being acted upon)[1] and a natural, spiritual intelligence as the seed of our personality. As such, our potential for greatness is immense.

Perhaps now you can see why I am so optimistic about our creative potential and why I try to see people as people – or even better, as children of God without any man-made labels, stereotypes, or categories. Perhaps now you can see why I try to be a good human, aspire toward greatness, try to see with the eye of faith, and crave congruence (or integrity) between belief and action. I truly cannot separate who I am, what I have helped to create, or how I have lived from what I know about God.

MY PURPOSE

This book is the culmination of years of study and conversations about art, creativity, teaching, and leadership. I have done much of this work in academic settings as a student, faculty member, or academic program chair. I have also completed professional development courses in leadership, including a certificate in Creative Leadership, from IDEO U – the educational arm of the design and innovation firm, IDEO.

The purpose of this book is to make creative leadership visible and viable for academic leaders and teachers. It is to inspire greater personal

[1] *Book of Mormon,* (The Church of Jesus Christ of Latter-Day Saints), 5.

awareness, fulfillment, and growth in all readers and encourage a culture of innovation in teams and classrooms.

I hope to be able to describe creative leadership in such a way that academic leaders can develop tangible ways to be more imaginative in their lives and leadership. This book is designed to support their professional development needs and is especially tailored to those who want to develop their own imagination and foster that same type of development in those they lead and teach. This growth will happen as they learn to integrate the proper mindsets, explore and implement visual thinking strategies, and leverage creative tension to achieve their vision.

While the primary audience for this book is faculty and academic leaders in the higher education system, I am not sure I really need to make a distinction between faculty and leaders. I see faculty as leaders and innovators within their classroom and programs. I know that the principles I describe will help them design and implement new creative strategies for their unique challenges.

As I write about this ideal leadership approach, I will use terms or phrases that communicate confidence in this strategy. This is potentially problematic because you might come away with the impression that creative leaders are always creative, always achieving awesome results, and *never* getting lost in the reactive hum-drum of everyday academic life. This is not the case. But we are also *never* satisfied with the status quo.

Instead of feeling less creative while comparing yourself to other creatives, I hope that you will let go of comparison and pre-conceived ideas about what it means to be creative.

I invite you to see, embrace, and develop your full creative potential. Learn to live more creatively and lead with your imagination. I invite you to be a creative leader, one who maximizes the creative efforts and abilities of individuals and teams – and helps them translate their vision into reality.

IMAGINATIVE FUNDAMENTALS

The primary focus of Section I is to remind readers of their inherent creative potential, identify the power of core beliefs, and
define mindsets that foster creativity. We explore what it means
to be a creative leader, as well as the framework, vocabulary, and
benefits of creative leadership for academic leaders. This section
concludes with an invitation to choose creative leadership as a
powerful approach to leading others and translating collective
vision into reality.

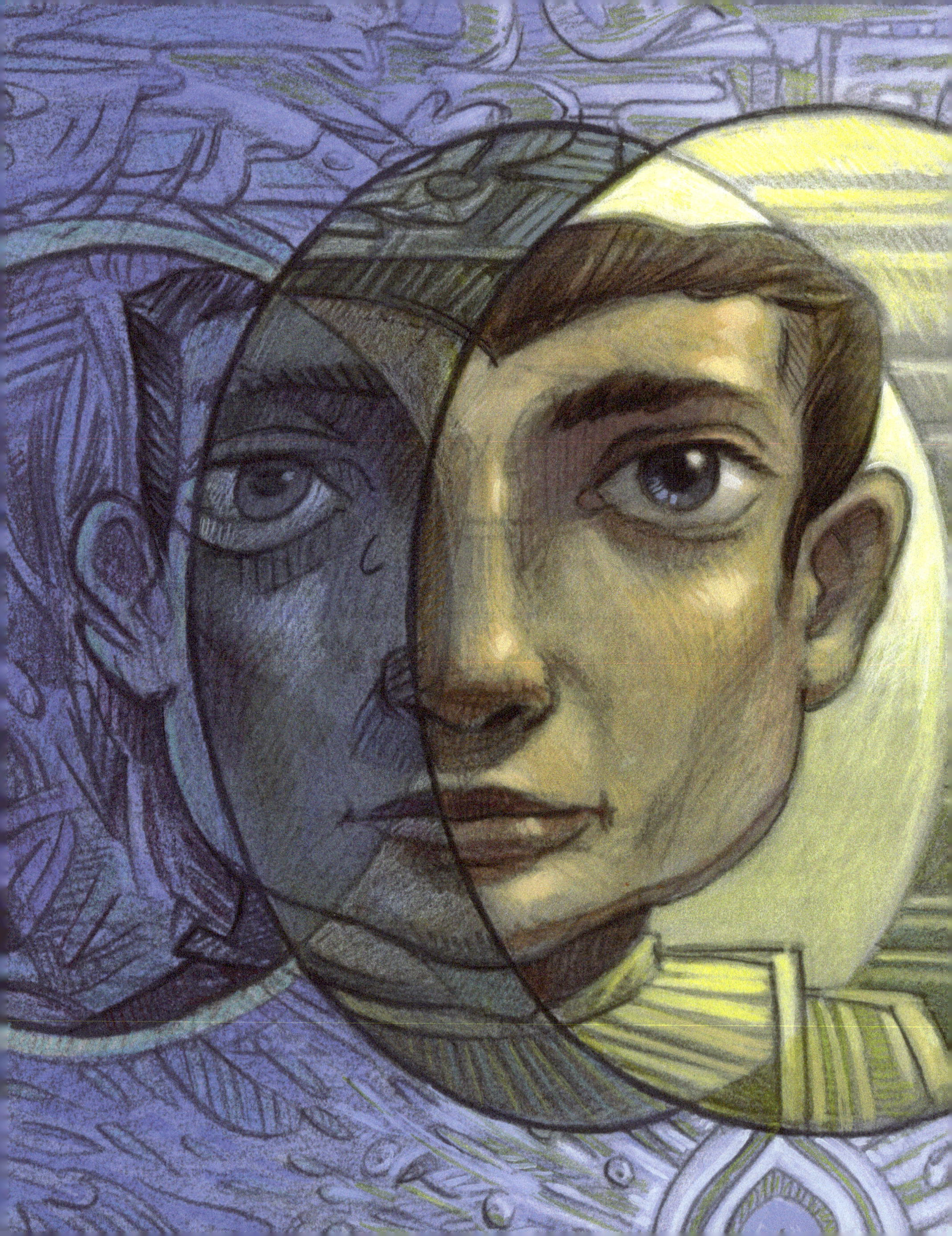

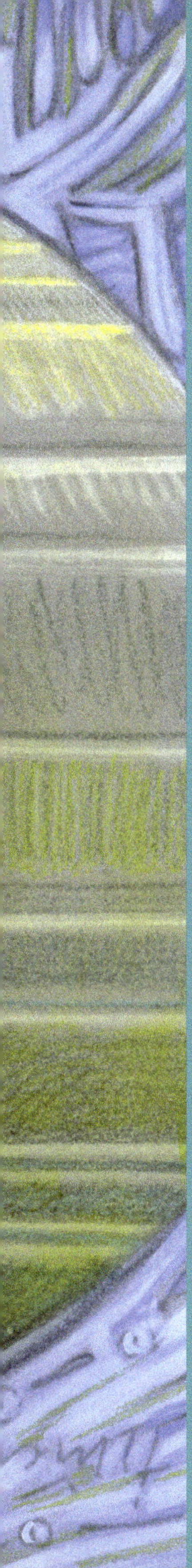

A STRATEGY FOR LEADERSHIP

As a young missionary in Portugal, I was put in charge of a group of about 20 missionaries. The mission was divided into groups called zones, and mine was "O zona de Luz" – the "zone of light." (It sounds way better in Portuguese!) I became responsible for the physical and spiritual well-being of each member.

This new sense of responsibility gave me a lot to think about. I *really* needed to know what leadership was, and fast! I woke up early each day to study – searching for understanding and enlightenment.

One day, I discovered a powerful quote about leadership. It was so important to me that I wrote it on the outside of an air-mail envelope and sent it home. The quote by Warren Bennis read, "Leadership is the capacity to translate vision into reality."[2]

This compelling quote was suddenly an answer to my questions about leadership. In many of our missionary training sessions, our president said, "You have to get the vision..." for the work in your area – then he taught us how to do that. I knew, however, that getting the vision was only the first step. We couldn't stop there! We needed to somehow bring that vision into reality – as a group. I learned that leadership was not about me or what I wanted, it was about working with others to accomplish the vision.

Since then, I have used this quote often in presentations and discussions about leadership, including the day that I taught my visual thinking class about "vision." I explained that a vision is a clear idea or imagined picture of a future result – and *striving* for that vision is a powerful concept that drives us forward in the creative process.

During my career as a professional artist and an academic leader I have refined my understanding of both creativity and leadership. In the process, I realized something interesting about that quote I wrote on the envelope back in Portugal. It does not apply exclusively to leadership – in fact, it works best as a definition for creativity.

Creativity is the ability to translate vision into reality. Perhaps creativity and leadership have more in common than we think!

[2] Warren Bennis, https://www.rightwave.com/rwi/leadership-is-not-about-title-it-is-the-capacity-to-translate-vision-into-reality.

WHAT IS CREATIVE LEADERSHIP?

"Creativity" and "Leadership" are two of the most overused, misunderstood words in our vernacular today. Both seem hard to measure and difficult to define. They often get defined so broadly that they lose their meaning altogether. But what happens if we combine them!?

When combined, they become a unique approach to thinking, working, and leading that inspires growth and innovation. I call this approach: *Creative Leadership.*

This strategy is particularly relevant for today's academic leaders who work in a complex, restrictive culture that can suppress the imagination and make innovation difficult for individuals and groups. With Creative Leadership, these professionals can develop the imaginative and constructive abilities they need to overcome the status quo and translate their vision into reality.

This book will explore how to do exactly that – helping you develop tangible ways to be more imaginative in your life and leadership. Here, we will explore mindsets that foster innovation, how to integrate visual thinking strategies, and what it means to lead with your imagination. You will learn an approach to guiding others that synthesizes creative beliefs, thoughts, and actions into strategies that can help your group move through the creative process.

It is this idea of "vision" that brings leadership and creativity together. That is because translating vision is the essence of each. If you think about it, this is what artists do. They explore an abstract concept and then work to translate the idea into visual form. In a similar way, translating a shared vision is the essence of leadership. That is what creative leaders do. They develop and maximize the creative efforts and abilities of individuals and teams, helping them translate vision into reality.

WHAT IS A CREATIVE LEADER?

One day, while strolling around the school campus, I was introduced to a young lady considering our art program. We struck up a conversation and began walking together, as I explained some of the aspects of our program. She was stylishly dressed and had gotten many compliments from other students (people she had never met) telling her that they liked her outfit, especially her knee-high pink boots. At one point, she commented, "It's cool to see so many people not wearing regular clothes!"

Then she looked at my attire, and said: "Well, except you... but that's okay."

Yup! While I do consider myself creative, it doesn't show up in my clothing choices. Some people seem to have a wild eccentric style in mind when they think about what creative people wear. But I don't fit the societal mold of an out-of-the-box thinker, since my red Vans are possibly the most stylish thing I own. My "box" (closet) is mostly conservative grays and blues, with a few patterns here and there.

But that is my point – there is no "mold" for creative people or creative leaders. You can be creative without wearing expressive clothing. I mean, really!? Can you imagine a creative person trying to fit themselves into some type of "creativity mold," fashioned by comparing themselves to other creatives? It just doesn't make sense.

No, my vision of a creative leader is not about outward appearance, it's about embracing your inner creative voice. It is not about holding a particular degree or leadership position, it's about how you think. It is not about working a creative job within the creative economy – it's about leading an imaginative life and helping others create results that matter.

The four key ideas below will help you see my vision of a creative leader. It starts with the imagination.

Leading with Imagination

Creative leaders manifest their imagination in many different ways, but in all cases, their ingenuity stays close to the surface. In fact, it becomes their approach to life and work. They do not leave their imagination at the door or only use it in some contexts – it is always present. Sometimes evidence of their imagination is seen in artistic expression, making things, or creative problem-solving. And beyond these more obvious creative endeavors (or actually, by synthesizing them), a creative leader is particularly focused on leading themselves and their teams toward a powerful, collective vision. They bring all the skills of a visionary person together toward learning, innovation, and breaking the status quo in meaningful and purposeful ways.

Leveraging the Creative Process

Creative leaders are able to identify, explain, and leverage the actions, emotions, and ideals that are typically present in the creative process. They are particularly effective at choosing (and then creating) the results they want. For example, they develop an original vision and use the discrepancy between their goal and their current reality as creative energy – propelling them toward their dream. They do not shy away from the hard work of creating and they are not stifled by fear.

Creative leaders have fun with the creative process. They play! They open themselves up for the state of flow that comes in the midst of their leadership practice and find great satisfaction in adapting, designing, or improving.

Embracing Ambiguity and Collaboration

One quality that leads to a creative leader's success is patience, a powerful multiplier in every creative process. They can be especially patient with themselves, with risk, with practice, and with others. They allow themselves to try, fail, and grow. They allow the process to unfold.

Because of their patience, creative leaders have an outstanding ability to collaborate. And might actually *enjoy* the ambiguity (the messy stage) that seems to happen in nearly every collaboration. They attract and then lead people who want to engage in projects that require innovative and unique solutions. They have a deep respect for the creators of the past and recognize that building on their previous contributions is another form of collaboration. They might even embrace their perceived competitors as potential collaborators.

Designing for Success

Later in the book, I will describe the differences between the design process and the creative process. But for now, it's enough to say that creative leaders have an intuitive sense for the design process and when to employ it to reach their vision. Like any good designer, they know how to research and when to just go with their gut. They know when to diverge in their thinking and how to converge around the best idea.

Creative leaders know that success is not an accident; instead, it is by design. It is the result of understanding design principles, balancing form with function, asking the right questions, and practicing empathy for the end user. They know that every successful design will meet the needs of the intended audience – and they are able to leverage the unique power of their team to accomplish effective designs that solve critical problems.

WHAT DOES A CREATIVE LEADER DO?

Up to this point in the introduction, most of what I have described is a broad summary of the ways in which creative leaders think. This should give you some idea of the philosophies and strategies that they embrace and employ in their work. But you might be wondering, what does a creative leader actually do?

With their imagination fully engaged, creative leaders take steps that are designed to accomplish their vision, or that of their team. Their methods can be organized into three expansive actions. The word "expansive" is used to indicate that there are limitless situations in which creative leaders can apply these actions. Broadly speaking they: 1) develop vision, 2) close the gap, and 3) lead for innovation.

Develop Vision

One distinction that separates creative leaders from other leaders is their ability to develop a clear vision. They look past what is and imagine what could be. In other words, they can see beyond the conventional results of leadership and envision more rewarding outcomes for their group. And it's not *just* that they can imagine and clearly define the results they want – they are also able to harness the power of creative tension to bring that vision into being. They understand systems thinking, are practiced in design thinking, and regularly use visual thinking strategies for improved communication.

Creative leaders have learned that when they make an idea visible, it can be analyzed, understood, influenced, and ultimately created. So, they often use drawing (sometimes as a metaphor, often as a method) for making it visible and giving it form. They also use stories, symbols, and metaphors to help others see what they need to see.

If we were to go inside the mind of a creative leader, we would be able to identify a handful of beliefs, mindsets, or ways of thinking that support the innovative nature of their work. They think creatively, yes (i.e., unique and novel ideas); but, more specifically, they think about structure, systems, process, and design. Creative leaders have trained their imagination to see things that others don't. They see the big picture, the context, and the systems at play.

Close the Gap

With a defined vision in place, it is natural to sense a gap or discrepancy between that vision and our current reality. That gap creates tension, like pulling a rubber band. When you put energy into defining a vision, you stretch the rubber band, and effectively load the system with potential energy that wants to be released. This tension can be motivating, but it might also be overwhelming. And there are only two ways to resolve it – we can give up on our vision, letting the rubber band snap back into a state of rest. Or we can accomplish our vision and free ourselves from the tension.

Creative leaders close the gap – they accept the tension and make the vision real. Instead of giving up, the creative leader leverages the tension (caused by the gap) as motivation or energy to act. They act in spite of uncertainty, risk, and inertia. They know that their current situation (as good, bad, or difficult as it may be) has a lot of inertia because it is real, tangible, etc. And their idea of the future, no matter how clear or exciting it is, will require them to overcome the status quo, push off the weight of *"what is,"* so that they can create what *"could be."*

Closing the gap means doing the actual work of creation. It's not about visualizing or sketching anymore – it's about creating tangible results. In the process they learn to make effective, vision-based choices that move them closer to their goals. They choose their desired outcome over circumstance. They choose the right people, processes, resources, and tools to accomplish the work.

Lead for Innovation

Creative individuals can develop a unique vision and accomplish it largely on their own. That is one indication of their creative ability and it may manifest through different forms of personal expression, like making art. Creative leaders, on the other hand, lead others toward impactful and significant innovations. They know that their purpose as a leader is to achieve innovative results with their team. They have learned how to leverage questions and facilitate great ideas that will mobilize a group toward surprising and effective solutions.

Some academic leaders and institutions advocate for creativity and innovation, but then stifle it with an oppressive culture that honors the status quo. In contrast, creative leaders design culture and establish structures that lead to innovation. They do this by expecting creative results, celebrating the imagination, and giving others space to step back from the day-to-day and innovate their future. Their program or classroom becomes a rich seedbed for creative ideas as they challenge their team or their students to engage their imagination.

In short, leading for innovation means making space for new ideas and influencing others toward creative success. It means striving with your group to move beyond incremental change and reach for an ambitious collective vision. Creative leaders are always leading for innovation.

Innovation in Higher Education

Well, look at that. We are only a few pages into the introduction, and I have already managed to invoke a third overused, and highly ambiguous term – "innovation." What exactly does that mean? And why are creative leaders interested in innovation? Is there even a place for that in the traditional halls of academia? For me, innovation is the result of creative effort that has led to something unique or novel, unexpected or surprising. But I am not talking about innovating for the sake of change, for show, or to validate someone's job. The change needs to be useful and meaningful; it needs to be a result that matters.

And I am not talking about incremental change or continuous improvement. There is value in that, but true growth does not come by managing the day-to-day. It comes by striving for something great – something that is currently beyond our reach. It starts by developing a vision with our teams that will activate their imagination and potential.

One primary reason that I work in Higher Education is because I am inspired by *potential*. When I walk into a room of students and academics, I see immense creative potential. I see intense engagement in the type of education that inspires personal growth and innovation.

But even in the same room, I see people at risk of becoming demoralized and stagnant, getting dragged down by boredom, rigid structures, and exhausting limitations.

The absence of creative leadership limits growth and stifles the imagination. But leading your group toward innovation will help them reach their greatest creative potential. As you implement creative leadership, you will prompt growth in those you lead by developing their vision and helping them close the gap.

THE FRAMEWORK

We have briefly introduced the three expansive actions of a creative leader. We will address these further in later chapters. But for now, you have a preliminary sense for what creative leadership is, and what a creative leader does.

It would be impossible to proscribe, predict, or even categorize all the inputs and outcomes of Creative Leadership. It is far too comprehensive and organic for that. The ways that it can be applied are as varied and expansive as our imaginations!

But because it is so flexible and widely applicable, it may be difficult to pin down. The concept is simple… just lead with your imagination – but like a powerful engine driving us toward our destination, we may not understand exactly how it works. We can see exciting results and feel the energy it produces, but might not consider what is happening on the inside.

One way to understand the inner workings of an engine it is to take it apart – examine each component within the system, and then put it back together. (Just don't lose the screws!) Like a mechanic, we will disassemble the engine of creative leadership and see how each part works together in unison to drive innovation. We will separate and identify the component parts, analyzing each of them before bringing them back together in the final chapters.

In an effort to make creative leadership visible and help leaders reach their greatest potential, I have developed what I call the *Creative Leadership Framework*. The following visual will illustrate the interrelationships and complexities of creativity and leadership that are merging into a new way of working, thinking, and leading.

In this chapter, we will see how imagination provides the basis for all creative leadership, we will explore how three different thinking methods can empower our imagination, and we will learn how to synthesize concepts into reality using the three expansive actions. All three levels compound and interrelate with one another forming a basic framework that will be elaborated on throughout the book.

The Fundamental Level

The foundation of the Creative Leadership strategy is composed of our imagination and our core beliefs. The imagination is fundamental because it is the source of new ideas. It powers our creativity by helping us define and work toward a clear vision.

However, the imagination is bound by our core beliefs – represented here as a band that encircles the imagination. As we will explore in future chapters, the expression of our imagination is truly only limited by our own mindset – or fundamental beliefs. Our core beliefs will restrict or expand our imagination and dictate how much we bring it into our work and other activities.

At this fundamental level, the imagination can expand infinitely in every direction as you choose to embrace it, develop it, and lead with it. It will expand as you embrace a growth mindset, choose to be less reactive and more creative, or choose to flex your creative muscles. On the other hand, your creative potential is reduced if your core beliefs cause you to shrink, operate with a fixed mindset, or become too concerned with extrinsic motivations and reactivity.

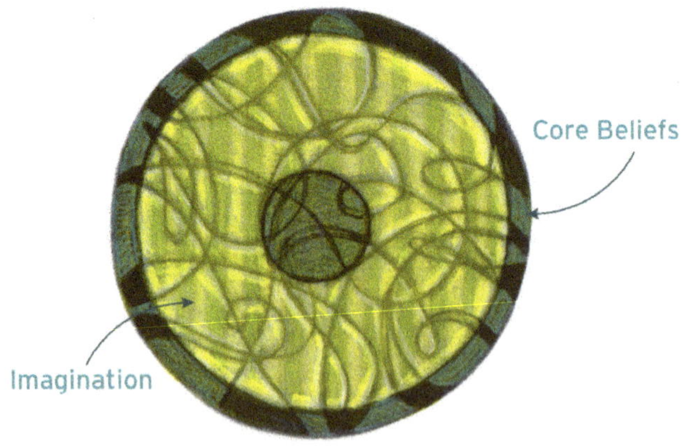

THE FUNDAMENTAL LEVEL

The Strategic Level

At the strategic level, we can use various thinking methods or processes to develop our leadership strategy. When visual, design, and systems thinking converge to guide your decisions, a highly creative personal leadership strategy emerges. Your imagination will be engaged and empowered. The results will be meaningful and exciting! You will find great joy in the creative process and in manifesting your imagination.

It should be noted that each component of the framework operates independently or distinctly. These are not steps or phases. This is not the design process or the creative process. Picture these thinking strategies as lenses through which you can view your work and your activities. When you are confronted with a problem, evaluate it through the lens of the strategic level and consider it from various angles.

Each of these thinking strategies will be discussed in greater detail in later chapters. By analyzing the problem through each lens, we will start to see it differently and a solution will soon become clear.

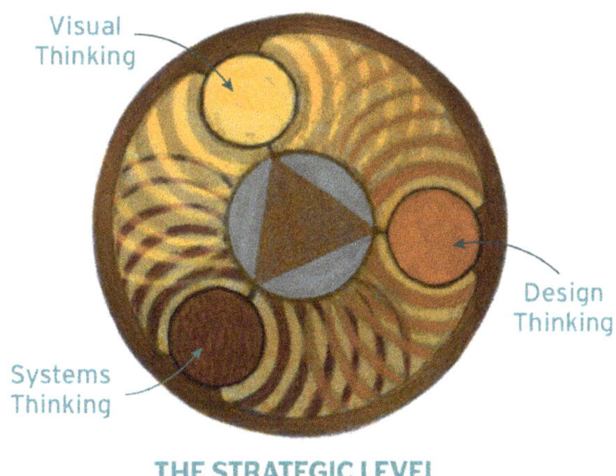

THE STRATEGIC LEVEL

- Are you clear about the system within which the problem is manifesting itself? (see Systems Thinking, Chapter 6)

- Is the issue calling for a collaborative session to design a solution? (see Design Thinking, Chapter 10).

- Is there a way to draw the problem so that others can see it and help you understand it? (see Visual Thinking, Chapter 12)

The Synthesis Level

With the tools and thinking methods of visual thinking, design thinking, and systems thinking informing our strategy, we are ready to synthesize all of the levels to achieve creative results. We are ready to apply our imagination to every situation and decision. Saying we are "ready," however, makes it sound like we have to wait to synthesize until we have fully understood or used every thinking strategy. As the word synthesis implies, it can be a simultaneous integration of each level into creative action. We don't have to wait!

In the introduction, you were introduced to three categories of expansive creative actions that manifest themselves at the synthesis level. These actions – develop vision, close the gap, lead for innovation – have a relationship with and are affected by the fundamental level and the strategic level. As we synthesize (or, in other words, become a creative leader), our imagination and thinking strategies will affect all of our actions and decisions.

For example, the expansive action of *developing vision* relies on the imagination at the fundamental level. It can be part of a design thinking strategy and will manifest itself at the synthesis level as helping others to develop vision.

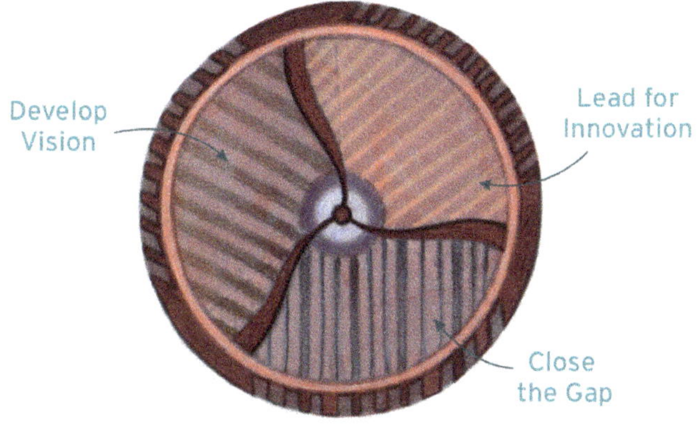

THE SYNTHESIS LEVEL

Organizing the Discussion

This chapter has presented a visual representation of an organic, comprehensive approach to leadership. This framework will also serve to organize our discussion of creative leadership. Accordingly, the book is divided into three sections: Imaginative Fundamentals, Thinking Strategies, and Creative Synthesis.

In the first section (Introduction to Chapter 5), we describe our individual and collective need for creative leadership. We introduce the vocabulary, expansive actions, and conceptual structure of creative leadership. The goal of this section is to help you recognize your inherent imaginative abilities and core beliefs. With that as a foundation, you can choose creative leadership; a fundamental approach that is built upon the imagination and expanded by mindsets that foster creativity.

Section 2 (Chapters 6-13) is all about strategy. Creative Leadership strategies are framed by an understanding of the creative process, creative vision, and the design process. We explore visual thinking strategies (such as design thinking) that creative leaders utilize to lead their groups through the creative process, building creative momentum toward accomplishing their shared vision.

The third section (Chapters 14-20) describes how creative leaders use effective teaching and a culture of innovation to lead others toward closing the gap. We discuss creativity at the synthesis level as the fusion of creative beliefs, thinking strategies, and expansive actions that creative leaders employ to lead others toward accomplishing their vision. As we complete our discussion, leaders are invited to manifest creative synthesis as they influence, develop, organize, and maximize the creative efforts of their teams, helping them translate vision into reality.

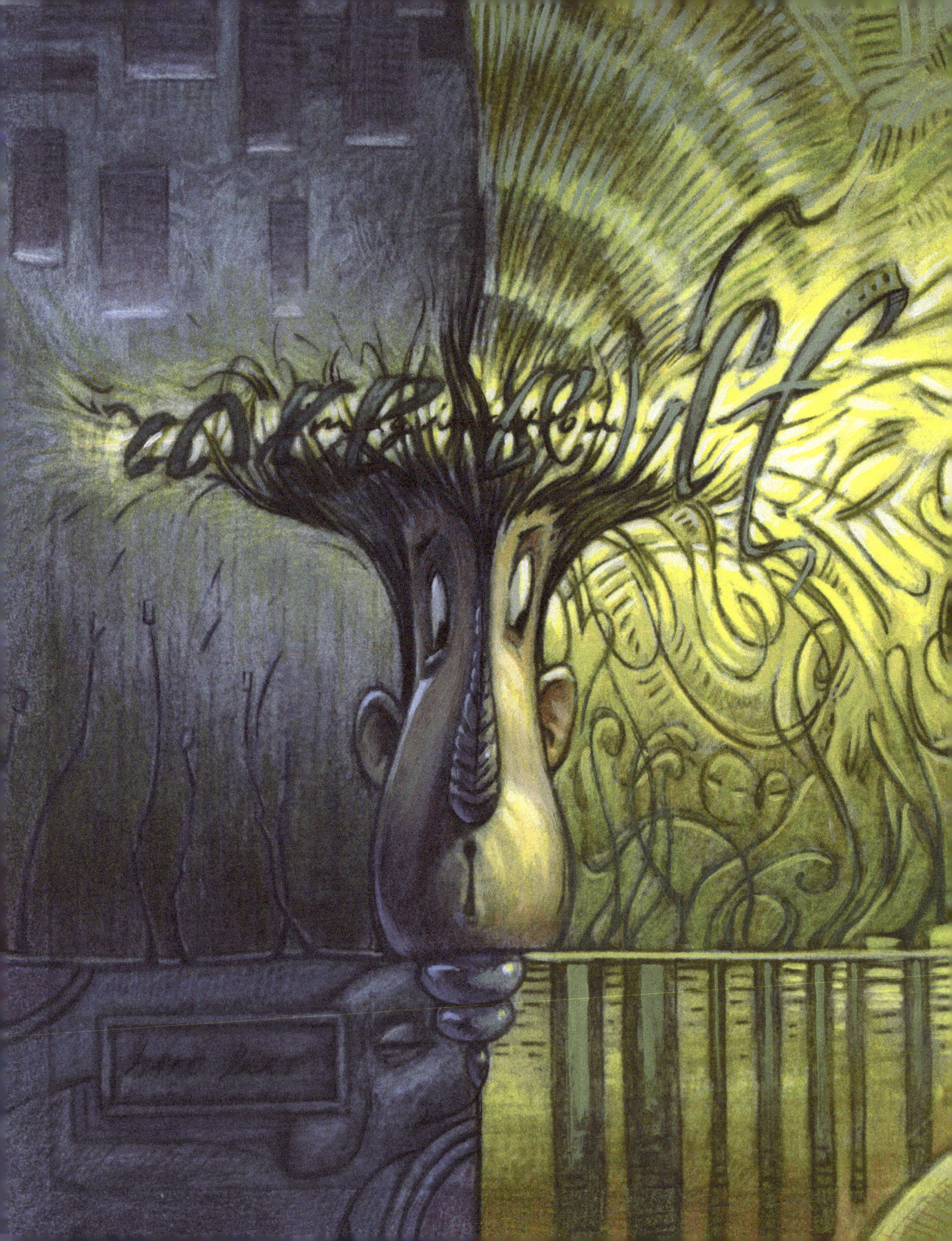
yourself

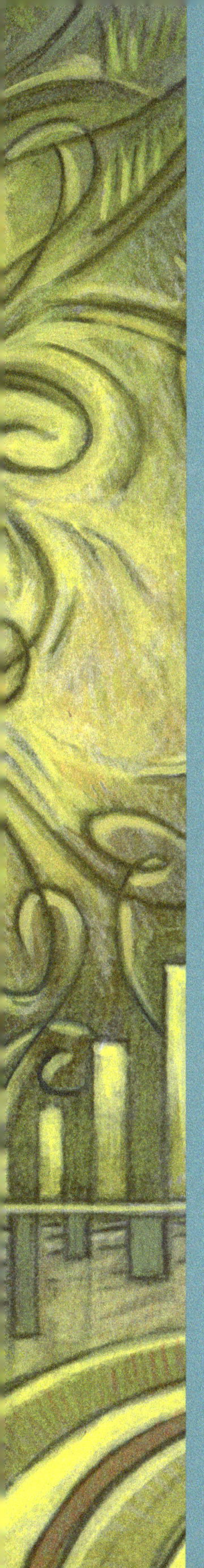

CHAPTER I

YOU ARE *ALREADY* CREATIVE

One day, I was conversing at lunch with some of my highly creative and talented colleagues at the art college where I work. We were laughing with my friend who had just purchased a paint-by-numbers project and was attempting to complete it. She thought it might be a good way to relax after work. The problem was, she couldn't see the numbers. They were too light and too small! Lacking the confidence to make up her own color scheme, she simply set it aside.

In response to this idea of painting by numbers, the conversation shifted, and we started talking about "being creative." We discussed what it means to be creative and if it was a quality we identified with. The sentiment that three of my colleagues communicated was: *"Yeah… I don't really consider myself creative."*

What!? These are professional academic leaders who use their imagination every day to solve problems for students! Have we established such a high standard for creativity that very few of us feel like we are meeting the mark? When did our definition of the word "creative" become so exclusive? We have been taught (and seem to believe) that creativity is a gift that only some people have. That high honor seems to be limited to those who manifest their talent and creativity in *certain* artistic ways, such as art, craft, music, dance, etc.

In fact, *all* people have immense creative potential – whether they recognize it or not. You *are* creative! I can almost guarantee, however, that some of you just tilted your head to one side, squinted one eye, and thought to yourself… *"Me? Creative? I don't think so…"*

It might take some time for us to let go of years of perceptions and messages about what it means to be creative. Many of us have developed a very narrow understanding of the word and have concluded that we do not fit society's creative mold. *This needs to change.* I am not suggesting that we tear up the foundations of our creative disciplines and rethink societal labels altogether – we just need to change our core beliefs.

CORE BELIEFS

Your core beliefs about yourself (and others) will *limit or expand* your inherent creative potential. If you believe that you lack some kind of innate quality or talent – that will limit your innovative output.

However, if you believe that your imagination is a gift that should be used and can be developed, your creative potential will expand. This is because our beliefs are a powerful catalyst, they influence our world more than we recognize.

The idea of creativity applies to all circumstances where the imagination can manifest itself. It is not limited to artistic endeavors alone. But I often hear the following from my "non-creative" friends...

"I don't have a creative bone in my body."
I cannot tell you how many times I have heard a statement like this. It is born of the belief that creativity is a unique talent, buried deep within a person – that some people have, and others just... don't.

"I can't even draw a stick figure."
This phrase is usually said after someone sees my paintings or learns that I am an artist. It is fostered by the idea that creative expression needs to be recognizable and believable. As an illustrator, I have spent years developing the ability to tell stories with representational imagery. But being able to draw a *stick figure* is not the only indication of creative potential.

So, if you have expressed this kind of belief before, please let it go! You were born with inherent creativity and great creative potential. You have been endowed with a powerful gift: an imagination. How you manifest your imagination is unique to you.

If you have trouble believing me, spend 30 minutes observing or playing with the children around you. This might take some intention, but the learning will be valuable. Children are powerful examples of humankind's innate imaginative character. Kids who are ages three to six are especially great at imaginative play.

You could also look to your own past to find examples of your own inherent creative power. Do you have any memories of playing in the backyard, or the basement, without a hovering adult or the TV screen? Did you ever turn a large cardboard box into a submarine or a spaceship? Or make a castle fortress with the couch cushions? Maybe you played "store" or "house" or acted out other activities like "dress up" or "cops and robbers?" These are all acts of imaginative play that indicate our inherent creativity.

One summer, when I was about ten, some friends and I discovered a large climbable tree in the vacant lot across from my house. We also found some old wood which sparked a flurry of creative activity. We decided to create a tree fort! We pooled our resources, rounded up some tools and spent days (or maybe hours) working in the tree. Our goal was to arrange and build a space for each of us to sit and relax. We never accomplished a roof, but each of us imagined our space and then used what we had to make a comfortable place high up in the tree.

I remember thinking how great it was going to be – once we got it all done – to just relax up there and hang out. It would be our perfect space: no chores, no parents, just us and the freedom of summer. But I think that lasted for about 30 minutes! Ironically, once we finished *making* our perfect space, we lost interest in it. I think we visited there periodically, but it was never accompanied by the intense creative play that we enjoyed as we were in the construction phase. We mostly went back to remember how cool it was that we built it. The fact that we naturally and spontaneously engaged our imagination, and then lost interest when the making phase was done, is an indication of our inherent creative drive.

CONSIDER YOUR CORE BELIEFS

In this chapter, I have asked you to look around (or to your past) for examples of humankind's inherent imagination. Having established that creativity is inherent in each of us, I invite you to examine your core beliefs. The word "core" is used to describe the type of belief that is deeply seeded in your mind and heart; even at your core. These beliefs are so deep that it's very possible that you have never articulated them or formed them as a conscious thought.

So, how do we examine something so obscure? Pay attention to what you *say*, as our words are often a reflection of what we believe. To consider your core beliefs, you could start by writing a list of phrases or ideas that you have expressed to yourself or others about your own creativity and imagination. Then identify where these thoughts are coming from. Are they based on your suspicion that you don't measure up in the creativity category? Following this line of thought will lead you to recognize the beliefs that seeded those statements.

Many of us have embraced our imagination and built artistic careers on empowering core beliefs. And many others have enjoyed the fruits of our creative expressions. But even those who are considered the most creative among us may struggle with limiting mentalities, based on core beliefs.

Fear is often another reflection of our core beliefs. Making or trying something new is often laced with risk. When we take risks, we feel fear (apprehension, anxiety, or avoidance). What are we really afraid of? And why does fear present itself? As you analyze your fears, you will be able to identify core beliefs that restrict your imagination. These types of fearful beliefs may have held you back when you wanted to share an idea, but then decided not to. Or when you created something but set it aside, afraid of what others might think. Fear is the great buzzkill for creativity.

The following quote by Marianne Williamson speaks about the influence of fear on our creative output:

> "Our deepest fear is not that we are inadequate. Our deepest fear is that we are powerful beyond measure. It is our light, not our darkness that most frightens us. We ask ourselves, 'Who am I to be brilliant, gorgeous, talented, fabulous?' Actually, who are you not to be? You are a child of God. You playing small does not serve the world. There is nothing enlightened about shrinking so that other people won't feel insecure around you. We are all meant to shine, as children do. We were born to make manifest the glory of God that is within us..."[3]

Are you afraid of your own brilliance? Have you forgotten how to play? Or is there some other fear that is limiting your creativity? We can learn much by exploring our preconceived notions about what it means to be brilliant, talented, or creative.

These notions may reveal fears, comparisons, and ideas about our not-so-creative past – the very reasons we have found ourselves asking:

[3] Marianne Williamson, A Return to Love: Reflections on the Principles of "A Course in Miracles" (1992), 190.

"Who am I to be creative?" or "Who am I to be artistic, imaginative, and to embrace my unique greatness?"

Who are you not to be? *You do not have to shrink!* We are all meant to play and create and imagine, as children do. We were born to manifest our imagination into the world. That is what I mean when I say, *"You are already creative!"*

UNSURE ABOUT HOW TO EXAMINE YOUR CORE BELIEFS?

Start here: You might remember the other day when you saw your friend working on a creative project. Maybe you said something like: "I could never do that!"

Step 1: Write that phrase.

Step 2: Pretend you are a little child and ask yourself a series of questions. They should all start with "why?" Answer each one honestly. Why did I say that? (Answer) Why do I think that? (Answer) Why? Why? Why?

If you follow this far enough, you should be able to identify the deeply-held beliefs that influenced your outward expression.

CHAPTER 2

CONTRASTING MINDSETS

When I was a freshman in college, the city asked me to create a large mural on a downtown building to promote a local dance festival. I created a 30 ft.-wide design that featured one of the beautiful dancers. She had her hands outstretched, as if she had just finished her performance.

The details are hazy now, but I remember my plan was to use an overhead projector to get the drawing up on the wall. The only problem was the placement of the projector. Setting it on a ladder on the sidewalk (my first plan) created too much distortion of the image. In the end, I borrowed a hydraulic lift from the school district, moved it into the middle of the street, and worked late into the night to establish the drawing. I then spent about two weeks painting and making multiple trips to the hardware store around the corner for paint.

I learned a lot as I completed the project and I enjoyed driving past it on my way to school. In time, we moved away and a few years later the mural was painted over. To this day I have yet to do another mural. In terms of my career, there was nothing significant about this project. But there are two remarkable things about this story. The first is that they chose me. Sure, I had done a couple of small projects in high school and the cover art of my yearbook. But if they had looked at my portfolio for evidence of large-scale murals, they would have found nothing. I was extremely unqualified for something of this scope.

But the second remarkable thing is this: I never questioned my ability to do the project. That was not confidence based on experience; it was an attitude (based on a core belief) that I would use my imagination to figure it out. And I did! I was able to achieve this new feat because my core beliefs oriented toward creativity. Confidence in my imagination had expanded my creative potential.

This story highlights the power of our core beliefs to affect our attitude or mindset – and the reason we should examine and carefully adopt beliefs that help us accomplish our vision. Moving forward, the word "mindset" will be used to describe a collection of attitudes, dispositions, or responses to any given situation. A mindset is an established approach, orientation, or a perspective.

Our mindset can become a positive guiding principle that leads us to meaningful creative results. But because they affect everything, positive mindsets should be carefully chosen and established. Unproductive mindsets can and should be dropped. If you want to change your mindsets or attitudes, you have to address them at the fundamental level – you have to choose better core beliefs.

Over the next few pages, I will describe four examples of contrasting mindsets. These mindsets can be described or plotted on a spectrum, but it is easiest to speak about them as opposites or contrasts.

FOUR CONTRASTING MINDSETS:

- Proactive versus Reactive

- Intrinsic versus Extrinsic

- Abundance versus Scarcity

- Growth versus Fixed

That's because there is a dichotomy between each opposing mindset and a suggestion that one side is more creative or open, and the other side is more close-minded or limiting.

PROACTIVE VERSUS REACTIVE

In 2007, I read a book by Robert Fritz that fundamentally changed my life. That sounds pretty dramatic. It wasn't dramatic or instantaneous, it was simple. The book influenced my core beliefs, changed my mindset, and helped me understand the creative process at a different level. Because of this book, *The Path of Least Resistance,* I began to move from reactive ways of thinking to a creative orientation or mindset.

Thinking in a reactive way seems to be the opposite of thinking in a proactive or productive way. Robert Fritz teaches that the creative mindset is a way of thinking that "is completely different from reacting or responding to the circumstances you are in..."[4] After all, you cannot create a ceramic pot, a new scientific theory, or the effective culture of an organization by accident. It takes intentional proactive work.

Escaping a reactive mindset is a choice. And when we choose to be productive – instead of reactive – we can overcome our present circumstances and create the results we want. Robert Fritz explains that most of us live our lives within the reactive-responsive orientation

> **...FOR THOSE FACING DIFFICULT STARTING CIRCUMSTANCES... FOCUS ON WHERE YOU ARE HEADED AND NOT WHERE YOU BEGAN. IT WOULD BE WRONG TO IGNORE YOUR CIRCUMSTANCES – THEY ARE REAL AND NEED TO BE ADDRESSED. BUT OVER-FOCUSING ON A DIFFICULT STARTING POINT CAN CAUSE IT TO DEFINE YOU AND EVEN CONSTRAIN YOUR ABILITY TO CHOOSE.**
>
> – Clark Gilbert

[4] Robert Fritz, The Path of Least Resistance (New York: Fawcett Books, 1984), 48.

(mindset), the complete antithesis of the creative orientation. Our energy is spent reacting or responding to outside influences and circumstances instead of creating our personal vision.

While it is important to acknowledge our circumstances and recognize our limitations – they do not have to dictate our present attitudes or our future results. Many people develop a victim mentality (and negative attitude) when it appears that the forces around them are conspiring against them; while others (i.e., creative leaders) study their current reality carefully, envision a better future, and begin making the decisions that will get them closer to their goal. That pattern of thinking is part of the creative mindset.

When I was teaching my students about this dichotomy, I thought it would be helpful to assess my own mindset. I asked myself, *"Where do I stand on this continuum between the proactive and the reactive?"* To answer this question, I made a list of decisions or behaviors that might indicate my motivation or mindset at work. On one side I listed things I did that felt proactive. On the other side, I wrote down things that appeared more reactive.

REACTIVE	PROACTIVE
Focus on short term fixes, i.e., the quick hire.	Plan effectively for the long term; take time to hire the right person.
Procrastinate hard decisions, i.e., waiting for someone else to make the call.	Go find the information you need to be able to act; take responsibility.
Create an artificial timeline and then decide to do the project myself.	Delegate with patience; develop leadership or growth in others.
Protect the status quo.	Be an agent of change; embrace change.
Procrastinate; only meet deadlines under pressure.	Plan ahead, work ahead, anticipate deadlines and needs.

Looking at my daily work and decisions in this way, helped me to identify those times when I was reacting to or being controlled by circumstances, as well as the times when I was approaching my work with a creative mindset. With this review, I was able to avoid reactivity and increase the time and energy I spent in the creative orientation.

You might be thinking, but how are "reactive ways of thinking" and "a creative orientation" mutually exclusive? Can creative action not also be a reaction? To a degree, yes. We can act in creative ways in response to our circumstances. But the distinction I am making here has to do with our core beliefs. An "orientation" is based on our beliefs. It is the default view or frame of reference that influences our thinking.

With a reactive or responsive orientation, we wait for circumstances to tell us what to do. But when we develop a proactive mindset, it is our own vision that becomes our frame of reference and the primary driver of our action. We are not controlled by circumstances but can acknowledge the circumstances and choose to move toward our vision.

INTRINSIC VERSUS EXTRINSIC

Another book that reinforced this concept of living within the creative orientation, looks at it from the standpoint of motivation. Daniel Pink, in his book called *Drive,* describes two ways of thinking that parallel the proactive and reactive orientations that Fritz described. Some of us are motivated intrinsically (creative) and others extrinsically (reactive). He called them Type I (Intrinsic) and Type X (Extrinsic).

Type I behavior:

"A way of thinking and an approach to life built around intrinsic, rather than extrinsic, motivators. It is powered by our innate need to direct our own lives, to learn and create new things, and to do better by ourselves and our world."

Type X behavior:

"Behavior that is fueled more by extrinsic desires than intrinsic ones and that concerns itself less with the inherent satisfaction of an activity and more with the external rewards to which that activity leads."[5]

Again, I decided to analyze my actions, this time evaluating my motivations. Think about your own actions and what they say about your motivation.

TYPE X (EXTRINSIC)	TYPE I (INTRINSIC)
Make a quick decision because of outside pressure.	Take time to research and evaluate. And then stay with a decision long enough to see it through.
Respond to pressure to answer every email or take on every project (people-pleasing).	Communicate effectively and intentionally; reach out, talk to people in person.
Perform for the institution, the boss, the executives, or the board.	Be student-focused and motivated by their success and needs.
Make decisions based on circumstances, exceptions, or feelings.	Use objective, vision-based criteria to make decisions.

Are you more focused on circumstance or vision? Are you motivated by outside pressure or intrinsic desires? This will help you see (and possibly shift) your orientation. Moving toward intrinsic motivations will keep you focused and help you move toward your vision despite the pressures that are happening all around you.

[5] Daniel H. Pink, Drive (New York: Riverhead Books/ Penguin, 2009), 77.

ABUNDANCE VERSUS SCARCITY

When Stephen R. Covey wrote about mindsets in his book *The 7 Habits of Highly Effective People*, he used a different word with a similar meaning. He used the word "paradigm" to describe a mindset, a group of attitudes, patterns of thinking, or character traits. Notice also how he describes the effect of core beliefs on our mentality.

> "Most people are deeply scripted in what I call the Scarcity Mentality. They see life as having only so much, as though there were only one pie out there. And if someone got a bigger piece of the pie, it would mean less for everybody else. The Scarcity Mentality is the zero-sum paradigm of life."[6]

This paradigm or mindset is extremely easy to fall into. Resources are finite and competition is fierce. But if we aspire to lead creatively, we have to let go of scarcity. That is because the opportunity to bring our vision into reality is founded on the idea that there is space for something new, different, or better to be envisioned and created.

With scarcity, your belief will not allow you to envision a better future or improved results. Scarcity will stop you before you start. There is simply not enough to go around – and certainly not for you! The moment you desire more, the scarcity mentality will rise up and slap you back into your current reality. How can you imagine something better for yourself when everything you want is already owned or held by someone else?

If you take on a scarcity mindset, when someone else wins – you lose. This will put you in direct opposition with everyone around you

[6] Stephen R. Covey, The 7 Habits of Highly Effective People (New York: Simon & Schuster, 1989), 250.

– even the people on your team or the students in your classroom. You can't see a way to develop, help, or encourage them because they are your competition. They will take your piece of the pie!

Covey explains a better way to think:

> "The Abundance Mentality, on the other hand, flows out of a deep inner sense of personal worth and security. It is the paradigm that there is plenty out there and enough to spare for everybody. It results in sharing of prestige, of recognition, of profits, of decision making. It opens possibilities, options, alternatives, and *creativity*." (emphasis added)
>
> – Stephen R. Covey, The 7 Habits of Highly Effective People, 251.

The hopeful, optimistic, and developing nature of the abundant mindset leads to greater creativity. It will allow you to develop a clear vision and then close the gap. With an abundant mindset, you can let go of things like comparison, fear, and negativity. And letting go of these things is a prerequisite to maximizing your creative potential and building momentum toward your vision.

GROWTH VERSUS FIXED

Carol Dweck's book *Mindset: The New Psychology of Success* is a fascinating explanation of how the "view that you adopt for yourself profoundly affects the way you lead your life."[8] For the longest time, vehicle repair, sprinkler systems, and especially tree trimming were great mysteries to me. I would avoid maintenance or repairs until the car broke down, the sprinklers froze and erupted, and the tree died or lost

8 Carol Dweck, Mindset: The New Psychology of Success (New York: Ballantine Books, 2004), 6.

limbs to negligence and heavy spring snows. I had what Dweck called a fixed mentality, and did not see myself capable of learning these things. Dweck describes two contrasting mindsets:

Fixed Mindset

> "Believing that your qualities are carved in stone – the fixed mindset – creates an urgency to prove yourself over and over. If you have only a certain amount of intelligence, a certain personality, and a certain moral character – well, then you'd better prove that you have a healthy dose of them… You were smart or you weren't and failure meant you weren't. It was that simple. If you could arrange successes and avoid failures (at all costs) you could stay smart. Struggles, mistakes, perseverance were just not part of this picture…"[9]

Growth Mindset

> "There is another mindset in which these traits are not simply a hand you're dealt and have to live with… In this mindset, the hand you're dealt is just the starting point for development. This growth mindset is based on the belief that your basic qualities are things that you can cultivate through your efforts… everyone can change and grow through application and experience. …The passion for stretching yourself and sticking to it, even (or especially) when it's not going well, is the hallmark of the growth mindset."[10]

[9] Carol Dweck, Mindset: The New Psychology of Success, 4.

[10] Carol Dweck, Mindset: The New Psychology of Success, 7.

Over time (and partly out of necessity), I have learned to work with each of these household priorities. I have worked hard to change my orientation toward learning and adopt a growth mentality. Just one example will help me make my point.

When my Grandma purchased a more dependable vehicle, she "sold" me her old Buick for a dollar. It was a blessing to have a second car and it worked great for quite a while. We called it the "grandma car." On the way to Youth Night, I stopped to give some of the guys a lift to the church. When I saw them I hit the brakes and quickly threw the grandma car into reverse. I completely roasted the transmission! The old Buick limped to the activity and coasted back home but was essentially a lost cause. I could not afford to replace the transmission on a vehicle that was not worth the cost of a new transmission.

But a buddy of mine offered to help me fix it. We went to the junkyard and he showed me how to check the fluid to see if the transmission we found there was still good. He showed me how to drop out the new one, and how to lift the rest of the engine while we replaced the transmission. I mostly handed him tools while he worked, but the experience completely demystified the process of car repair. If I can change out a transmission, I thought, I could easily do more than change a tire or check the oil.

This event prompted me out of my fixed mentality. Instead of feeling stuck or limited by circumstance or lack of resources, I have learned to replace the brakes on multiple vehicles, swap out a radiator, a couple of alternators, the timing belt, and spark plugs, etc.

The growth mindset is inherently creative and leads to innovative results. This is because the imaginative ideas and constructive skills you need to accomplish your vision are not fixed, they can be learned.

AN INTERESTING PARADOX

Putting the words "growth" and "mindset" together seems like an interesting paradox. While "mindset" conveys a certain aspect of being fixed, it is set; "growth" means it is not set but evolving. I believe that our mindsets can evolve and change. Adopting productive core beliefs will profoundly affect the way we live and lead.

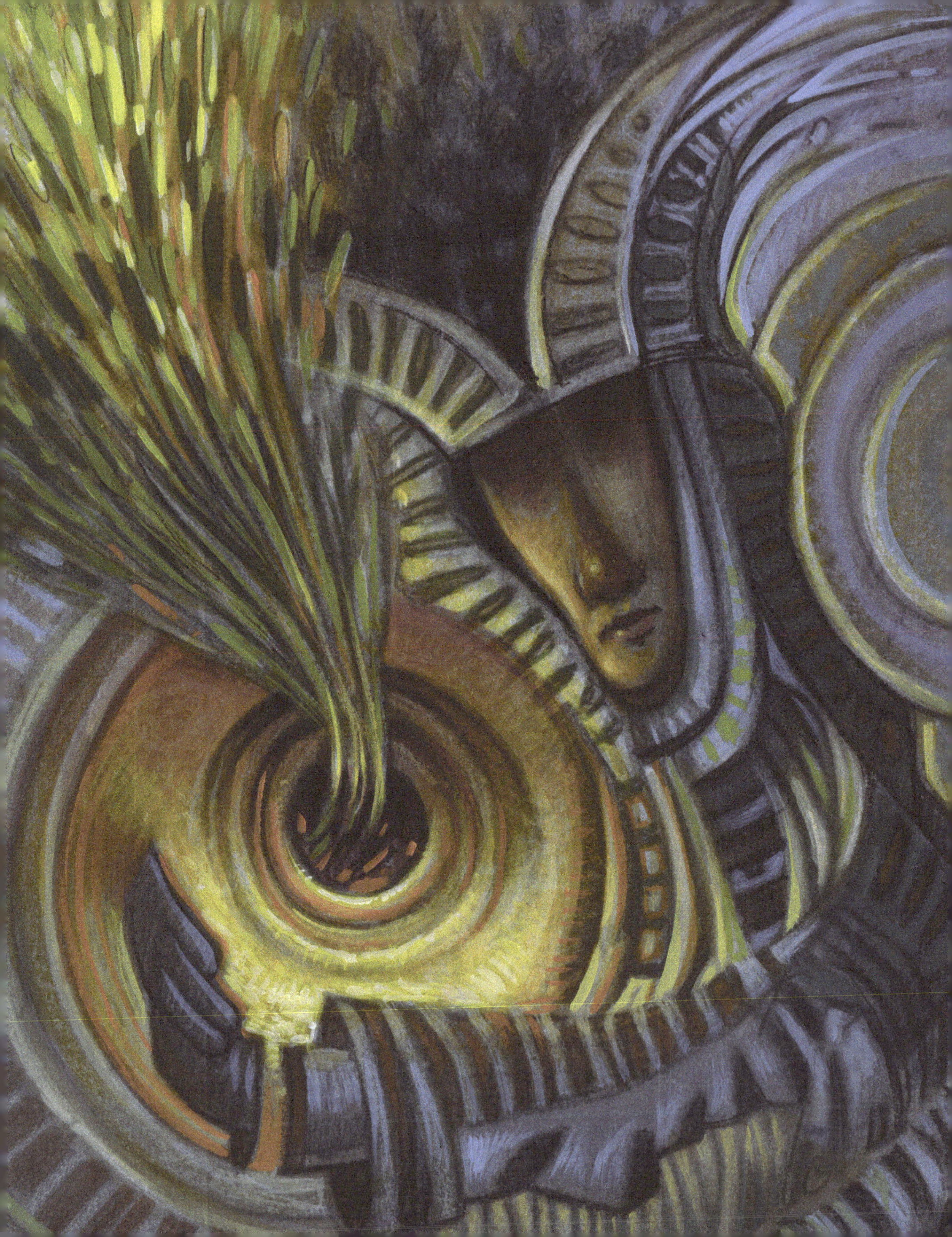

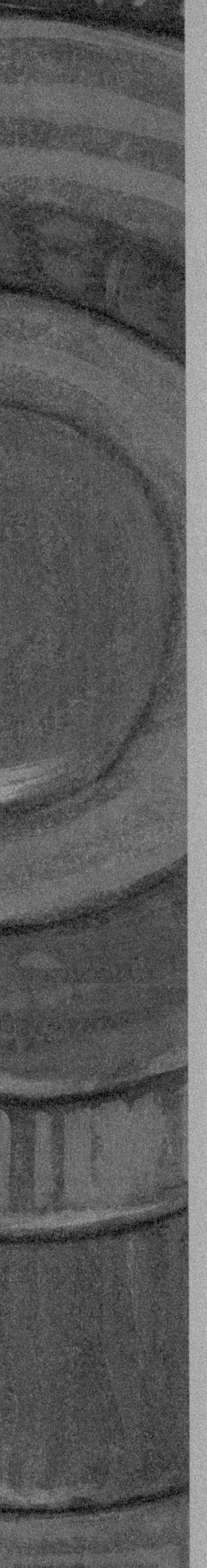

CHAPTER 3

EMBRACE THE CREATIVE MINDSET

With an introduction to each of the contrasting mindsets, you are invited to consider which mindsets you hold and how they may be influencing you. If you find yourself limited by reactivity, extrinsic motivations, scarcity, or fixed ideas about your ability to learn, you can work to transition to the creative mindset. Choosing a new frame of reference or attitude toward imaginative work will strengthen your ability to translate your vision into reality.

The following statements exemplify the creative leader's approach to life, teaching, and leadership. They are founded in beliefs about creativity, intrinsic motivation, abundance, and growth that you can choose to adopt and believe about yourself. Choosing them will establish productive mindsets that can dramatically increase your creative disposition.

I am creative and lead with my imagination.
You can call yourself creative. You really can! But if that word is too heavy, or ambiguous, think of yourself as imaginative, open-minded, or design-oriented. With intention, you can develop the imaginative and constructive skills that you need to achieve innovative results. To lead with your imagination means that you bring your inherent abilities and new ideas into the work of guiding others. It might also mean that your imagination is your leading consideration – your guide.

I have power over my life and circumstance.
The opposite of choosing power over circumstance is a reactive mindset. When we are caught in that trap, it is easy to blame others for our situation and hand over our power of choice to the oppressive will of circumstance. We accept what we see as the inevitable and feel powerless. Or we believe that we are victims of an unfair system that is ruling over us.

I know there are exceptions, but by and large each of us have significant freedom and power over our own life. You can begin to believe that power over circumstance is possible. The first step is to choose this statement as part of your mindset. While we cannot always choose the circumstances we are thrust into, we can always choose our attitude about those circumstances.

I can imagine a better result.

Once we believe that we have some power over our life and circumstances, we can begin to imagine better results and better circumstances. Our imagination may be somewhat dormant after years of neglect, but it is still there – ready and waiting to be used. By imagining a better result we can kindle a spark of hope that will ignite and power our engine toward a better future. As with most initial actions, there is some resistance and sluggishness to overcome. Don't get discouraged if progress is slow. As we continue to fuel our imagination – even if results are imperceptible at first – we will begin to create the results we want to see in our lives and organizations.

I can see with the eye of faith.

I am aware of a verse of scripture that describes people who saw the object of their faith manifested before their eyes. They "truly saw with their (physical) eyes the things which they had beheld with an eye of faith, and they were glad."[11] Embedded in this verse is a beautiful concept that relates to our ability to envision a better future. In this context, the eye of faith is what makes our vision of the future so tangible to our mind's eye, that we can "see it" before it actually exists. We can envision the results we want with great clarity, *before* we create them.

I choose to lead with creativity.

As you might have understood, choice and belief are inextricably connected. You can choose to believe. And your core beliefs will affect all of your choices. As you choose to believe in your own creativity and power over circumstance, you can also choose to lead others with creativity. You can make creativity your focus. When you walk into the conference room or the classroom, you can honor and embrace the imagination above other considerations. When you lead with creativity, you are valuing ingenuity, design, and original thought.

[11] Ether 12:19, Book of Mormon (The Church of Jesus Christ of Latter-Day Saints), 509.

If you can truly believe and adopt these statements (or others like them), your work and leadership will be founded on core beliefs that will expand your inherent creativity. This will increase your capacity to lead yourself and your group to meaningful results.

Having identified some of the core beliefs that will support creative leadership, you might wonder if it is really that simple. Can you simply choose a new creative mindset? Can we really develop greater creativity? Of course! It is just like any other characteristic or skill – like patience, humility, or learning to draw. But first you must believe that this is a choice you can actually make. That is why we addressed the idea of core beliefs and mindsets in previous chapters.

If you have not already chosen creativity as a driving force in your life, you can choose it now. Embrace your creative drive by choosing core beliefs that foster imaginative thoughts and actions. Life is too short to spend much time in a reactive mindset, feeling victimized by circumstance. Adopt the creative mindset and create results that matter to you. Accomplish your vision!

The creative mindset that fuels creative leadership has the potential to bring us deep satisfaction, but each of us has to choose it. Creative results don't just happen, they are chosen.

You can choose creativity – and by extension, creative leadership as your approach to leadership. There is great joy in engaging your imagination, reaching toward your highest potential, and helping others do the same.

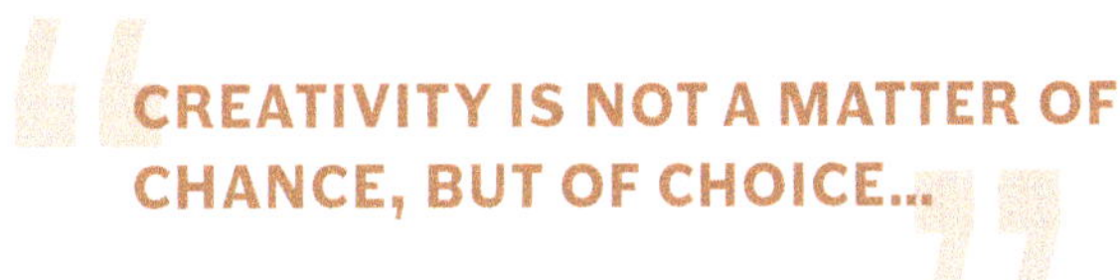

– Robert Fritz

In the rest of this chapter we will define creativity, explore what it looks like when we manifest our imagination, and then discuss leadership in the next chapter. By the end, you will be ready to commit to this expansive strategy.

CREATIVITY

Let's define creativity. Creativity is the imaginative and constructive ability to translate vision into reality. Someone with this ability can harness the power of their mind and the work of their hands to create a new form or experience. This requires critical thinking skills founded on effective core beliefs. It takes practical skills to organize, craft, or develop an abstract concept into a tangible form or experience.

Your imagination is the source of your ability to form new ideas or concepts, and to envision something that does not yet exist or is not present. When you create, you give tangible form to an idea that had only existed in your imagination. In a way, you have *realized* your imagination. And this new form becomes the evidence of your imaginative and constructive skills – it's the evidence of your creativity.

These new forms, like fruits of a harvest, sprout from the seeds of our imagination growing into something new, becoming real. We can then see, feel, or experience the results of creativity or what I call the "Manifestations of the Imagination."

MANIFESTATIONS OF THE IMAGINATION:

1. Artistic Expression

2. Making Stuff

3. Problem Solving

4. Innovation

Artistic Expression:
Many people can envision and harness the great communicative properties of various media such as poetry, music, humor, dance, images, and theater. When we use these mediums to transcend language and develop new avenues for communication or symbolic expression, we have engaged our imagination in artistic expression. Using our imagination, we can develop new avenues of meaning and learn to use symbols, metaphors, and various media to express new ideas.

Making Stuff:

Making Stuff (for lack of a smarter sounding title) is another manifestation of our imagination. We can envision and then make something new. Sometimes, we are not interested in communicating anything at all, we just want to make it. We create just because we enjoy the process. Or we might make it for its function. Artists, artisans, and builders all make stuff. Handmade furniture and décor, products, sculptures, and buildings are all examples of this category.

Problem Solving:

The imagination is highly valued for its ability to solve problems. And everyone, from the smallest child struggling with a new game to the experienced scientist wrestling with mathematical theories, can employ the imagination. We act creatively when we develop or improvise new solutions, processes, strategies, or designs to solve our problems.

Innovation:

To innovate is to create something novel, yet relevant; unexpected, yet meaningful. And as humans, we value this. We like things that are new, unique, surprising, or different. We like new products that change the status quo. We can appreciate artwork that diverges from tradition in dramatic ways. We enjoy a unique perspective and a novel solution.

I would suggest that individuals who manifest high levels of creativity are able to implement aspects of each of the above categories into their innovations. They don't just express themselves but do so in a way that communicates a clear message or intent. They don't just make stuff but make stuff that is of high quality. They don't just solve problems, but they solve the right problems in effective ways. Lastly, they don't just radically innovate in divergent ways, but their innovative contribution is effective and... unexpected.

But here's a question: Is there a hierarchy of creative manifestations? Are some types of art or expression more important or more "creative" than others? *I don't think so.* We will learn about the end user in the chapter on design, and how they will naturally assign value to our designs or creations. But the apparent manifestation of our vision is still, by nature, creative – even if it is not valued as such.It should be considered creative because it is a clear expression of our imaginative ability and creative vision.

– Michael Bingham

But what if the use of our imagination is never recognized as creative? Does the product or result have to be recognized as such (by an outsider) for it to be considered creative? Mihaly Csikszentmihalyi, a professor renowned for his work on creativity seems to suggest this. He said:

> "Creativity occurs when a person, using the symbols of a given domain, such as music, engineering, business, or mathematics, has an idea or sees a new pattern, and when this novelty is selected by the appropriate field for inclusion into the relevant domain."[12]

[12] Mihaly Csikszentmihalyi, Creativity: Flow and the Psychology of Discovery and Invention (New York: Harper Collins, 1996), 27.

There are a number of problems with this explanation of what it means to be creative. To begin with, it seems to spring from a reactive mindset. By this definition, all of us have to wait for an outside system or entity to notice, approve, and select the *occurrence* of our creativity into the domain. Additionally, this way of thinking breeds extrinsic motivation and sets a discouragingly high standard for what can be considered creative. This is far too exclusive for the holistic definition I have provided here.

In stark contrast, the definition of creativity we espouse as a creative leader is all-encompassing. It includes all manifestations of the imagination. It embraces each person's unique ability to use their imagination to achieve creative results. This definition helps to identify creativity (in myself and others) and the types of thoughts that lead us to novel results.

It might be important to note that we may be using our imagination very well in particular circumstances, and less well in others. Depending on various factors, we may be confidently creative at home, but then feel limited or uninspired at school or work. It takes practice and intention, but we can learn to be imaginative in every situation. The next chapter will explore simple ways to think and act more creatively wherever we are.

CHAPTER 4

CHOOSE CREATIVE LEADERSHIP

If you do the hard work of consciously choosing core beliefs that foster creativity, creative thoughts and actions will naturally occur as a result of those beliefs. Those actions and thoughts will be indications that you are developing a creative mindset. But beyond addressing our core beliefs at the fundamental level, what can we do to develop our creativity?

The answer is simple – create. Use your imaginative and constructive skills to bring the vision into reality.

Creativity is based upon two types of skills – imaginative and constructive. Both can be intentionally developed. Imaginative skills are thinking habits like questioning, diverging, and imagining. Constructive skills are practices like sketching, making, and solving.

IMAGINATIVE SKILLS

Many times, when we reflect on "creative thinking," we imagine energetic brainstorming sessions, wild ideas, novelty, invention, and intense moments of discovery, etc. This has a tendency to set our expectations pretty high. We might stare at the blank canvas, or the whiteboard and feel like our ideas or efforts will never measure up.

There is a less dramatic approach to creative thinking that is more common and honestly, more fruitful. Let's call it: *"thinking toward creation."* This means that we have a vision of what could be and are working through a process to envision, design, and then create it – as opposed to trying to pull a finished concept from thin air. Obviously, "it" is whatever you want to manifest, from a very tangible object to an ethereal experience. With this process in mind, creative thinking may

OUT OF THE BOX:

Sometimes people think about creativity as stepping "out of the box," moving beyond the constraints. And sometimes that is what it means. But I have found a greater need for imagination and creativity within the box (or structure) where the constraints are clearly defined.

include learning, assimilating skills, testing theories, studying resources, resting, etc.

Creative leaders choose the thinking models, strategies, or patterns that will help them *think toward* the creation of their vision. In later chapters, we will discuss some of these strategies in depth, including systems thinking, design thinking, and visual thinking. For now, here are some of the basic habits of creative thinkers: question, diverge, and imagine. Highlighting them here will give you some quick ways to develop and implement your imaginative skills.

Habit 1: Questioning

Creative thinkers are curious and so they ask questions. Their questions start with "why?", move to "what?", and finally to "how?" Our "why" questions are aimed at understanding our current reality, or the decisions that led to our present situation. It is important to question the status quo, the premise, and the context. "What" questions help us understand what is needed and what could be. "How" questions lead us to a plan or a path forward. The order of these questions (and the intent of the questions) is instructive.

Habit 2: Diverging

One distinct characteristic of creative thinking is the habit of diverging. It has been called brainstorming, versioning, ideating, etc. In order to develop new realities, we have to be willing to explore, experiment, and depart from what has been done before. One key aspect of diverging is the exploration of a wide variety of ideas or possibilities. It usually means withholding judgment on your ideas and dropping them into the pool of consideration, no matter how crazy they seem to be at first.

Habit 3: Imagining

Everyone has an imagination. But "imagining" is a creative thinking habit that can be developed and strengthened. Imagining is forming a clear picture of a future result – a vision of what you want to create in your mind's eye. By definition, a habit is something that you do with regularity. How often do you let your imagination go?

With intention, you can improve in your creative thinking. You can learn to ask the right types of questions at the right time. You can develop your ability to explore and diverge. You can practice and strengthen the habit of envisioning what could be. In the end, this will help you to envision and to bring about creative results.

CONSTRUCTIVE SKILLS

Beyond our thinking, however, if we want to achieve meaningful results we have to take action. Let's call this *"working toward creation."* When we talk about people who do creative work or act in creative ways, we might be tempted to jump to the stereotypes – the messy artist creating in their studio, the mad scientist, or the temperamental musician in performance mode. But creative leaders know that even non-artists can develop constructive skills to help them create whatever they envision.

As described in the introduction, there are three broad categories or expansive actions that creative leaders might take. These include developing vision, closing the gap, and leading for innovation. Included in each expansive action are basic constructive practices, actions that help us give our vision some preliminary tangible form.

These will be discussed in greater detail, but for now let me illustrate two fundamental creative actions. If you want to start now and develop your constructive skills, you can begin by giving form to your ideas. Here's how:

Practice #1: Sketching
Start with sketching. For an artist, the act of sketching is used to develop and plan for a finished piece. It is one way of giving an idea or a concept some tangible, yet preliminary form. When I work with art directors on children's books, I send sketches to show them what the final image might look like. If my sketch is too loose or unrefined, they may not understand it. If it is too polished, they may feel like all the creative decisions have been made and there is little room for collaboration.

Striking a similar balance is important when leading our group through a creative process. As part of a creative leader's collaborative work, "sketching" means roughing in the plan, drafting some initial concepts, or outlining a process, etc. Creative leaders take time to consider rough concepts with their team instead of just laying down the final plan. They know that sketching will allow others to imagine the direction they would like to go and contribute ideas without getting hung up on details.

Practice #2: Prototyping

As we conceive of something and manifest it in some tangible way, we can feel a great sense of accomplishment. If the result truly matters to us, it makes it that much more joyful. Meaningful creation is often the result of a significant investment of time and resources, which can make it devastating when it doesn't work. Often overlooked, prototyping gives us a way to test our idea in a low-investment way before committing to the final form. We can learn a lot as we prototype our plans. Finding simple ways to prototype is a basic practice that will help develop your constructive skills and your innovative ideas.

With an introduction to the imaginative habits and constructive practices of creative leaders, we can now turn our focus to Leadership. Leadership is also skill that can and must be developed.

DEVELOPING LEADERSHIP

My understanding of leadership is based on my studies and personal experiences. I have studied leadership, worked with hundreds of leaders, and have been influenced by many more. I have been called a leader in a variety of settings. In the following section, I will use three ideas from James MacGregor Burns, an award-winning writer, as conceptual underpinnings for my definition of leadership.

Collective Purpose:

Burns wrote, "Leadership is nothing if not linked to collective purpose."[13] He called it collective purpose. I call it collective vision. This highlights my explanation that leadership is about guiding groups toward the translation of their collective vision into reality. This is also the distinction between a true leader, and someone who merely manages workflow and timesheets. A true leader will move us toward meaningful results and help us create a new reality.

Leadership as a Process:

Summarizing Burns' theories around leadership, Joanne B Ciulla, Ph.D., noted that his work may prompt us to see "...leadership as a process, not a set of individual acts." This view of leadership makes sense. Leadership, as a series of decisions and actions, serves to maximize the efforts of the group and helps them accomplish their vision. Perhaps that is why we spend so much time discussing the creative process and the design process in this book.

My vision of a leader is someone who can reveal and remove roadblocks, design structures, and create systems that will lead others through a process to creative results. Ultimately, they pave the path of least resistance for those they teach and lead.

Burns described two basic types of leadership – the transactional and the transforming. The relationship between leader and follower in transactional leadership is based the exchange of "one thing for an-

13 James MacGregor Burns, Leadership (New York: Harper Collins, 1978), Prologue.

other, i.e., jobs for votes". Transforming refers to the idea of developing leadership in others. He explained that transforming leadership is more complex, and it is also "more potent," meaning perhaps more engaging, satisfying, and demanding. "The result of transforming leadership is a relationship of mutual elevation that converts followers into leaders..."[14]

Elevating followers:

Elevating followers and helping them become leaders is both a means to an end... and the end. It can be a very effective way to achieve the vision, as well as part of the vision. Wherever the group is trying to go, they need to arrive there as better people, better leaders. It is not enough to simply lead others forward without developing them in the process. As leaders and teachers, we can play a critical role in helping others strengthen their imaginative and constructive potential – even their creativity.

As a society, we have put all sorts of qualifiers in front of the word – leadership, i.e., transactional, authentic, servant, even creative. This helps us to understand the unique aspects of this complex process. But at the end of the day, *effective* leadership is the one we are all searching for. In this book, effective leadership means bringing our team closer to accomplishing our collective vision.

With some understanding of how this complex idea and process of leadership is framed, (with the help of Burns) let's discover the fundamental beliefs of an effective leader. Implementing these three core beliefs will make effective leadership a reality for us and our teams.

[14] James MacGregor Burns, Leadership (New York: Harper Collins, 1978), Prologue.

Belief #1: I am guided by a set of fixed principles.

Effective leaders are also followers – if nothing else, they follow a set of core beliefs, values, or principles that are unchanging. Those fixed principles become a stable north star in a swirling universe of changing positions and conditions. That doesn't mean that it's the *leaders* who are fixed or unchanging. They are still willing to learn, change their minds, and grow in their understanding.

Rather, it means that their behavior is grounded in fixed values or beliefs. And those values are made apparent to those they lead. Living by an established set of fixed principles is a necessary part of effectively building trust with those we lead.

I believe that "there really is absolute truth,"[15] and certain things are simply right and constant, but that is not what I am saying here. I am suggesting that effective leadership is founded on trust and clarity – which happens when we are constant in our adherence to core values. The most effective leaders have integrity – a clear connection between their expressed beliefs and their actions.

Later we will talk more about how vision is critical for the creative leader. Since the vision is the objective, the end point, or destination, reaching for that destination is what guides the leader and influences their decisions. But it can't be just about the vision. It must be about people and about basic human goodness, morality, or ethics. In other words, how we act on the way to the vision, is just as important as getting to the vision. If our mission is the *"what we do,"* and our vision is the *"where we go,"* then our values are the fixed principles that dictate *"how we act"* as we do and go.

[15] Russell M. Nelson, Pure Truth, Pure Doctrine and Pure Revelation, (The Church of Jesus Christ of Latter-Day Saints, Liahona 2021), Speech.

[16] Joanne B. Ciulla, Ph.D., "The Personal Morality Of Leaders: The Problem Of Moral Agency In Burns' Theory Of Transforming Leadership" (Jepson School of Leadership, 2015), 2.

Belief #2: I respect the agency of those I lead.

The leader/follower (or teacher/student) relationship is naturally marked by an "unequal distribution of power."[16] The leader will naturally start with more influence because of their title, position, or experience. As such, it is important for the leader to respect the agency of those who are in a position to follow.

Agency is the capacity of a member in the group to act or exert power. An effective leader will activate the agency of that person by giving them power, often in the form of authority or responsibility. Receiving this power engages the member's interest in the success of the group. They become partners who act in the best interest of the group. As leaders empower group members to act and contribute, the group will surge forward toward their stated objectives.

In contrast, less effective leaders feel the need to control, maintain power, and limit the agency of group members. As a result, they gain influence by coercion, manipulation, and control (often confusing that influence with respect). Attempting to control is a form of influence, yes – but not the kind that motivates groups toward their highest creative potential. "No power or influence can or ought to be maintained [except] by persuasion, meekness...and kindness"- in other words, respect.[17] An effective leader will respect group member's time, perspective, experience, and identity.

Effective leadership is not a one-way street. A leader can only lead if someone else is willing to follow. This is a give/give relationship. And as the leader, you make the first move. You have to lead with respect (pun intended.) As you give power, you gain influence. As you give re-

[17] Joseph Smith, Doctrine and Covenants (The Church of Jesus Christ of Latter-Day Saints), 242.

spect, you earn trust. With trust, the partnership goes forward and the group can work toward their shared vision. Without trust, they will be hampered in their progress.

Belief #3: Followers have the potential to become leaders.
Delegating tasks or giving power to those you lead is not just about gaining influence or dividing up the work that needs to be done. It is also about drawing out the best qualities of those in the group. It is an invitation that can activate their imagination and leverage their current abilities. When we do that, the group goes farther, faster.

It takes effort, but we can learn to see creative potential as it exists in others, without labels, stereotypes, and misconceptions that seem to define them. To do this, we strive to see group members accurately so we can understand them. And at the same time, we try to see them with the eye of faith and catch a glimpse of their immense possibilities. With this more complete picture, an effective leader can determine the type of role or assignment that will simultaneously build on current skill, and lead to future growth in those they lead.

Spencer W. Kimball, an effective church leader, wrote: "We can help them grow by making reasonable but real demands of them." In contrast, some "...leaders have sought to become so omnicompetent that they have tried to do everything themselves, which produces little growth in others."[18]

[18] Spencer W. Kimball, "Jesus: The Perfect Leader" (Ensign, 1979).

With patience we can nurture a belief in their own creativity. We can teach them to express themselves in artistic ways, to solve problems, and to work toward innovation. We can show them how to manifest their imagination in a variety of contexts, including their leadership. Of course, this is strategic on the part of an effective leader. If the imaginative and constructive skills of members in the group are expanding, that means the group is developing their creative potential, which will ultimately get us closer to our goals. This strategy will also reinforce and add credibility to our other stated beliefs, because it is based on a deep respect for their agency and their inherent creative potential.

If you adopt and live by this core belief, you will see that growth in leadership skills is part of a follower's highest potential. One day you will look back and see that, "Leadership begat leadership. Followers had become leaders."[19] That will be a good day!

In the long run, how you approach your leadership is a conscious choice. I am describing principles so that, with understanding and intention, you can choose to become an effective, creative leader. When you do, you will be helping them achieve their greatest potential, as well as achieving your own.

[19] Joanne Ciulla, "The Personal Morality Of Leaders: The Problem Of Moral Agency In Burns' Theory Of Transforming Leadership", 2.

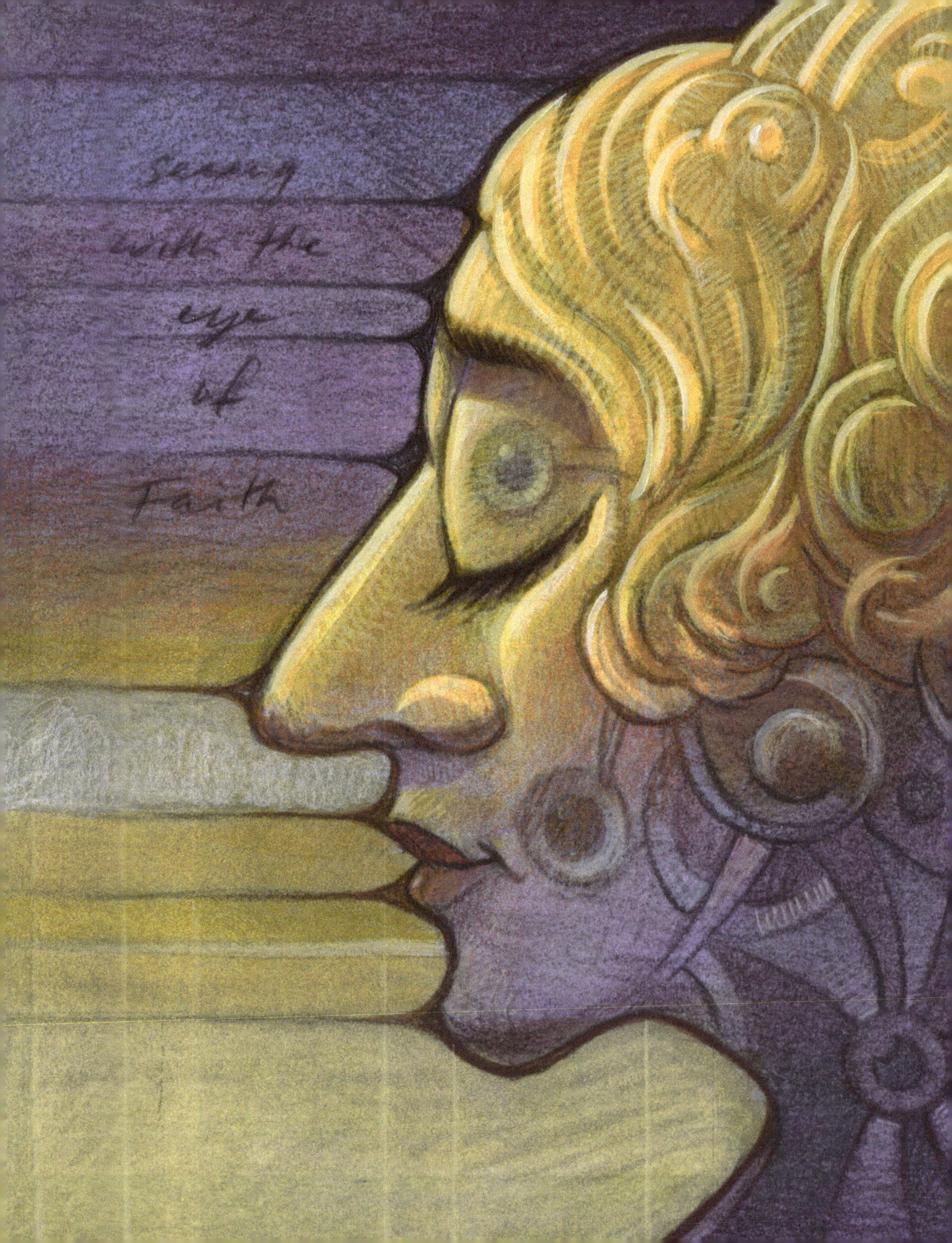

seeing
with the
eye
of
Faith

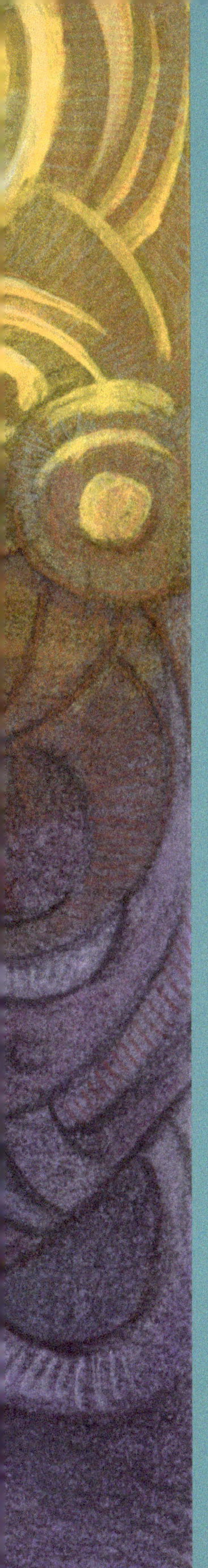

CHAPTER 5

SEE WITH AN EYE OF FAITH

The imaginative skills of a creative leader include the ability to visualize future objectives, conceptualize hidden structures or forces, and sense the gap between our current reality and what we want to achieve or create. This ability to see with the imagination is described in the framework as one of the expansive actions of a creative leader – there it is called "Develop Vision." This versatile action can be applied to every situation or decision we make within the creative process. It is particularly effective in moving our group forward as we establish our destination, find ways to visualize our progress, and recognize hidden currents that may push us off course.

As an expansive action (based on a fundamental imaginative skill) developing our creative vision also strengthens our use of visual thinking strategies. There are three types of visual thinking strategies found in the strategic level of the creative leadership framework: Visual Thinking, Design Thinking, and Systems Thinking. The next chapter begins our exploration of the strategic level by introducing systems thinking as one aspect of our creative vision.

Before describing this powerful strategy, it will be important to delineate the difference between "vision" and "creative vision." As described earlier, a vision is a clear idea or picture of a future result. It is our desire, objective, or destination. Creative vision, on the other hand, is the intellectual skill or ability to see hidden structures, define our objective (vision), and see the gap. It is called "creative" vision because this type of vision is particularly relevant within the creative process.

3 ASPECTS OF CREATIVE VISION:

- Seeing the future (what could be) with an eye of faith.

- Seeing the gap between where you are and where you want to be.

- Seeing the systems, structures, relationships, and components at play.

There are at least three distinct aspects of creative vision. The first is to envision the future (what could be) with an eye of faith. Using this aspect of creative vision, creative leaders engage their team to define what they really want. Having this clear picture of their goal will help them organize priorities and leverage structures to accomplish their vision.

The second aspect of creative vision is learning to see the gap between where you are and where you want to be. It is important to be able to see this gap so that you know how close you are to your destination. This is critical context for your team as you move through uncharted waters toward your vision. Without this clarity we might tempted to minimize the gap – thinking we are closer to our vision than we really are. This will effectively release the tension that would otherwise be pulling you toward your goals and it may weaken your resolve to achieve your vision.

To imagine and understand the forces, structures, and relationships within a given system or working environment is the third aspect of creative vision. An example from the artist's studio may shed light on this important skill. When an artist draws a still life of fruit, for example, their goal is to replicate the relationships of shape, color, light, etc., on the drawing paper. If they can get those relationships right, the drawing will look like the still life.

A common mistake, however, is to spend more time focused on their drawing, and less time observing, studying, and really *understanding* the relationships within the still life. When you can understand the relationships, you will be able to draw them accurately. In a similar way, creative leaders learn to see (and then draw) the relationships, structures, and systems that are affecting their group's progress. Studying these interrelationships allows creative leaders to identify and commit to a course of action.

DEVELOP VISION

So, let's talk about the first aspect – our vision of a future result. Simply put, the vision is a "clear idea of what could be." And it can be anything you want. It might be an idea, an ideal, or a desired outcome. You could call it a goal or an objective, but the clearest name for it is vision. And the clearer it is, the better. *We have to know where we are going.*

– Unknown

In this chapter, we will describe the benefits for creative leaders who spend time and energy developing a clear vision. We will identify some ways to develop it and make it visible to others. But first, let's explore what a vision is not...

Vision is not the process – Sometimes, if our vision is not clear, we might end up choosing the means to an end, instead of the result we want. If we are not careful, we might get caught up in the tool, or the software, or the procedure and forget (or never define) our vision.

Vision is not a mission statement – A mission statement clearly defines *what* we do; what business we are in. You could also think of it as a statement of purpose that describes why we do what we do.

Vision is not a value statement – A value statement highlights a character trait or noble ideal that we value and want to exhibit as a person or institution. Values are what we prioritize and how we treat others as we engage in our work.

Vision is not a belief, orientation, or mindset – On the contrary, our thoughts or beliefs inform our vision and open our mind to the possibilities.

Vision is not a purpose – There may be some overlap here, but purpose is broader than a vision. We can think of our purpose as our motivation or fundamental desire. Our purpose is the reason that we develop the vision and want to accomplish it.

Why develop vision?

One reason for developing a clear vision is pretty simple. If you want to create meaningful results in your life and your work, it starts with imagining those results. That is a universal principle. Without a clearly defined vision – you will likely find yourself floating aimlessly, being pulled by the currents that will take you anywhere and nowhere.

Choosing your harbor, will also help you determine and clarify your priorities along the way. This is because "...vision has power... [it] can help you organize your actions, focus your values, and clearly see what is relevant..."[20]

How to develop your vision

Developing your vision (by yourself, and with your team or class) is one of the most valuable actions you can take as a creative leader. It will help you get buy-in from your team and will establish a tension resolution system. But stepping back from the hustle and pressure of our incessant maintenance work to develop our vision may be hard to do. I mean, did you ever hear your boss say, *"You know, you should spend more time in reflection, envisioning what you really want to accomplish with this project. Take some time, and don't come in until Friday..."?*

[20] Robert Fritz, The Path of Least Resistence, 138.

The process of developing a clear vision will look different for each person – but here are some tips to consider.

DEVELOP A CLEAR VISION:

- Set aside time on your calendar for this type of work.

- Ask yourself, *"What do I really want?"* Listen to your gut, your intuition...

- Consider what you want, regardless of current circumstances. Be careful not to slip back into reactivity and think that whatever you decide has to fit within the realm of your current circumstances.

- Envision what you want, even if it doesn't seem possible. This is where your imagination comes in. You have to look past your weaknesses and limitations, and see potential.

- Engage your imagination with divergent thinking – brainstorm, record your impressions and ideas – lots of them! Withhold judgment of your ideas.

- Imagine and define the details of your vision. Engage your senses. What does it look like? Feel like? What will it be like when you have created it or achieved it?

- Make it tangible and concrete using words, pictures, symbols, etc., to make your vision visible to yourself and others.

Sharing your vision

A creative leader exerts positive influence and has the ability to create (or help others create) real, tangible results. But real, tangible results start out as abstract ideas – and it is pretty hard for people to help you create them when they don't have a clear idea of what you envision. This is why it is critical to make your vision *visible.*

If your team helps you to clarify and define the vision, they will have some idea of where the group is headed. But you may need to orient other stake-holders who were not a part of that vi-sioning process.

> **VISION IS EVERYTHING FOR A LEADER… WHY? BECAUSE VISION LEADS THE LEADER.**
>
> – John C. Maxwell

There are two common, low-tech ways to share a unique vision with those around you: 1) vision statements and 2) vision boards. Of course, there are many other ways to do this. Whatever you choose as a creative leader, one of your primary objectives should be to share the vision. This will help you clarify your objectives and motivate your team or your students.

CHECK YOUR WORK:

How will you know if you have an effective vision? Ask yourself, "Is my vision so clear that I will know it when I have achieved it?"

A vision statement is a written description of the vision. It does not need to have fancy words, but it does need to be clear and comprehensive. Reducing the idea to a single sentence or catchy phrase can be an important distillation process or communication strategy, it will help you refine and remember the core idea. However, a vision statement does not have to be short – it needs to be clear. It needs to be so clear that anyone can understand and envision the future results. It needs to be so defined that everyone can recognize when it has been achieved.

A vision board is a visual description of the vision. You can find or create pictures that represent the imagined results and place them on the board. You might not be able to capture everything into one image, or even a handful of images. So, don't be afraid to use a lot of images to clarify the vision for yourself or your team.

THINKING STRATEGIES

In this section, our discussion moves beyond internal mindsets and into the realms of process and strategy. Here the components of the creative process are introduced. We introduce creative tension and describe our first strategy – Systems Thinking. We highlight the importance of design, discover the design process, and explore Design Thinking as a mechanism to move past incremental change toward innovation. Visual Thinking is outlined as a powerful communication tool to engage the members of our group. Overall, this section describes how creative leaders use each of these disciplines to move their groups though the creative process and build momentum toward accomplishing their shared vision.

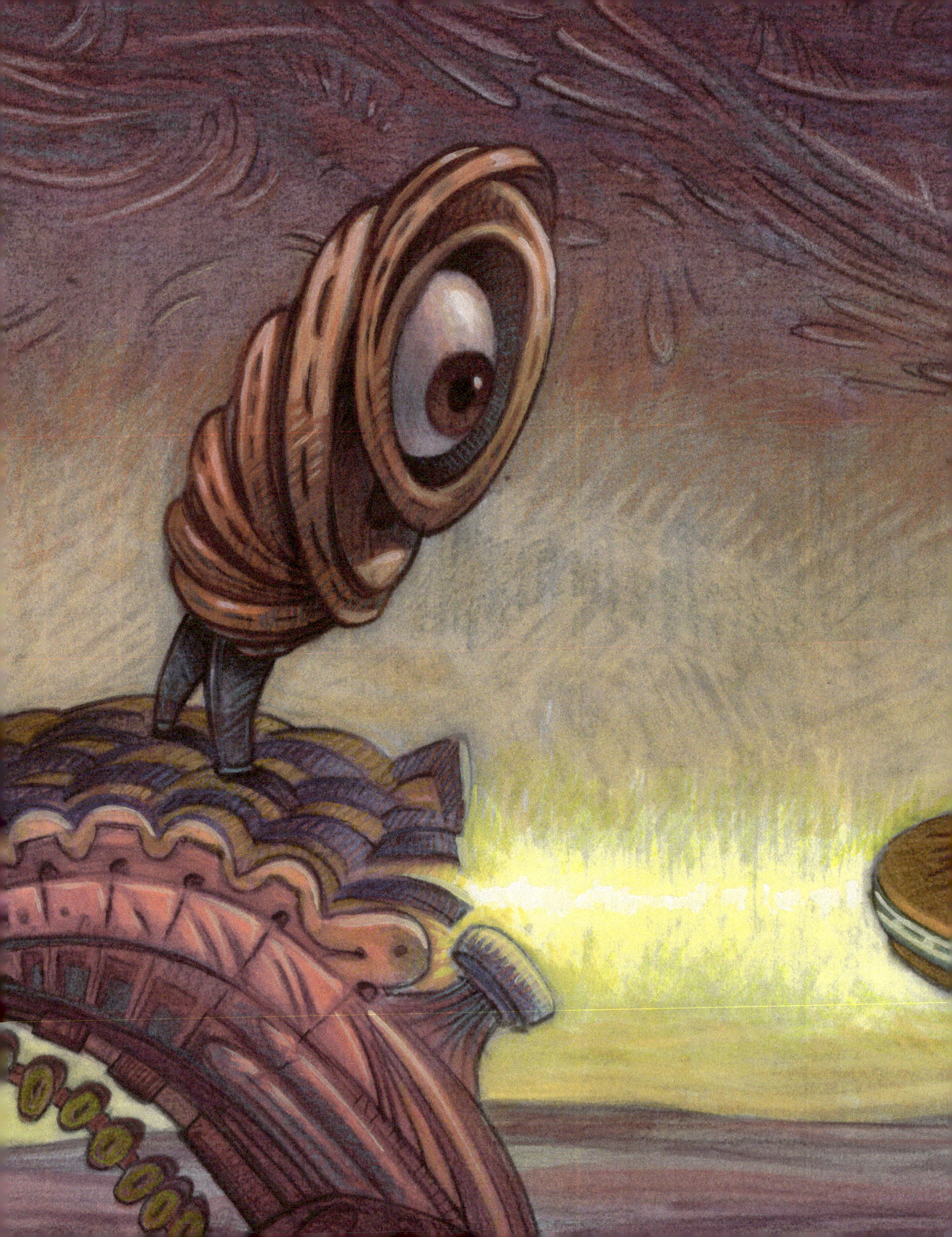

CHAPTER 6

VISUALIZE THE GAP

Up to this point, I have briefly introduced the idea of a gap or discrepancy between where we are (current reality), and where we want to be (vision). I had an interesting conversation about this with a colleague. We were discussing this idea of discrepancy. He suggested that it is one thing to deal with the discrepancy or the gap once it is identified, but it starts with being able to see the discrepancy in the first place.

I have seen this with my illustration students. At times, they don't know what else to do to improve their drawing or illustration. This might happen for two reasons. First, they did not spend the time necessary to develop a clear vision of where they were headed with their image. And without that vision, there was no perceivable gap. Secondly, they become satisfied with their work as is – so they don't (can't or won't) look critically at what they have made.

Like my students, if we are not truly objective about the work, we might misrepresent (to ourselves and others) how close we are to our vision. We might be tempted to say, "Yeah, this is basically what I was going for…" even when we are still far from our goal. This will have a tendency to minimize the gap and cause us to settle for less or compromise what we truly want. Separating our identity and our emotions from what we are creating and seeing it objectively is a critical skill for artists – and creative leaders.

To help the artist to see the relationships on the canvas with fresh eyes it is a good idea to step back, look away, or take a break from the work. They also may try using a mirror to look at the image, squint, or turn the picture upside down to see it objectively. When creative leaders step back and honestly evaluate their progress this will reveal new priorities and next steps. These ideas were not visible before because the leader had started to become too invested in and convinced of their own perception of current reality.

If we are partial and overly optimistic about our current reality, minimizing the gap is a real risk. But the opposite can happen as well. If we exaggerate the gap, we might think, "I am never going to get there… what I was hoping for is so far away!" This can increase discouragement and the temptation to quit. And if the leader falls to this sort of thinking, the team will certainly be demoralized and less effective.
To avoid compromising or losing hope, we just need to be honest as we

assess and communicate about our present circumstances. This honesty will help our group to see the gap accurately and objectively, so they clearly know where they are in relation to the stated vision. With that transparency, priorities will become clear.

SYSTEMS THINKING

In connection with the eye of faith, and visualizing the gap, the third aspect of creative vision is the ability to see and represent the forces, structures, relationships, and components that affect or influence our creative results. This is where systems thinking comes into play. Often, we are unaware of all the forces at play in a particular workplace culture or system. Systems Thinking is a strategy for identifying unseen systems – and making them visible.

Creative Leaders use their imagination to identify, analyze, and conceptualize the invisible dynamic forces within a system, often using visual symbols to help group members understand them. This way of thinking can be employed in a variety of ways and various contexts. It can be particularly helpful to apply when your group members are being held up by a system or structure they don't understand.

The example of a stretched rubber band that was used earlier is a simple system where the forces are obvious. But there are many other systems in our lives and our institutions that are much more complex. In my creativity class, when we discussed this idea, we would play the floating stick game.

In this game, participants have a simple task – lower the stick to the floor as a team. Seems easy enough, right? Three or four people stand opposite each other with their arms outstretched. They balance a long, light stick on their hands. And there is one basic rule – you have to be touching the stick at all times, but it has to rest on your hand – you cannot use your thumb or hold it like a baseball bat. Our participants come to learn that lowering the stick represents a complex system, with each participant's action representing an unseen force.

Lowering the stick takes communication and coordination among all the members of the team. And there are times when someone does not lower their hand at the same rate as everyone else and their hand loses contact with the stick. When this happens they raise their hand back up to the stick. If they overcompensate and push the stick up, it causes others on the team to also lose contact with the stick. If they over-compensate, the problem increases and the stick seems to rise involuntarily, instead of being lowered. The "floating" stick can be exacerbating, and fun! It is the visible result of an unseen system.

If you are a willing participant (in a game or at work), but unaware of how your actions can affect the outcomes of the group, you might be acting in a way that is contrary to the objectives of your team. You might be causing the metaphorical stick to float. Creative leaders use the discipline of systems thinking to identify interactions and describe what is *really* going on.

Peter Senge[21], author of *The Fifth Discipline*, is one such creative leader. He is known for clearly making the "system" visible to others. Using simple diagrams throughout his book, he describes complex systems using what he calls the Systems Archetypes. These archetypes are common dynamics that can be found in myriad situations and organizations.

Included here are brief descriptions of three of Senge's Archetypes:

Archetype 1: Balancing Process with Delay
"A person, a group, or an organization acting toward a goal, adjusts their behavior in response to delayed feedback. If they are not conscious of the delay, they end up taking more corrective action than needed, or (sometimes) just giving up because they cannot see that any progress is being made."[22]

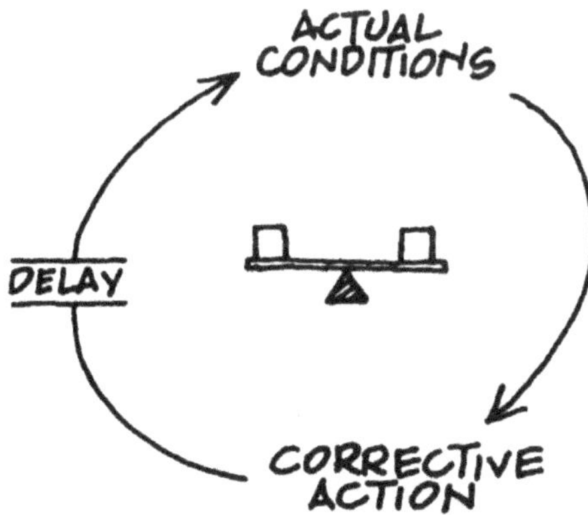

[21] I speak about two creative leaders in this section who have helped to define this discipline of Systems Thinking – Peter Senge and Robert Fritz. Their ideas seem to be connected. Senge credits Fritz by saying that "the principles and approach in The Path of Least Resistance have become a cornerstone in my work to help leaders and managers deal productively with complexity and change." Fritz has applied Senge's ideas of structural thinking to business as well, but his book is geared toward helping his readers become the dominant "creative force" in their own lives.

Archetype 2: Limits to Growth

"A process feeds on itself to produce a period of accelerating growth or expansion. Then the growth begins to slow, often inexplicably to the participants in the system…"[23]

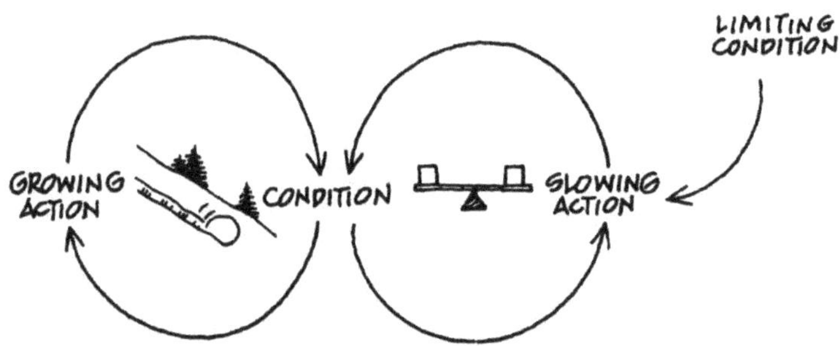

Archetype 3: Shifting the Burden

"A short term 'solution' is used to correct a problem, with seemingly positive immediate results. As this correction is used more and more, more fundamental long-term corrective measures are used less and less. Over time, the capabilities for the fundamental solution may atrophy or become disabled, leading to even greater reliance on the symptomatic solution."[24]

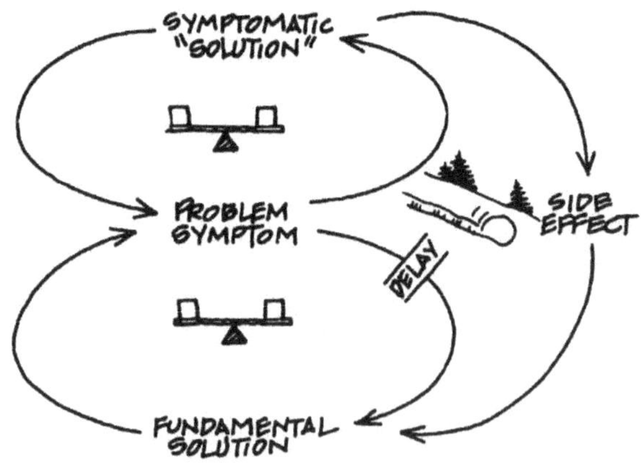

[22] Peter Senge, The Fifth Discipline (New York: Currency/Crown/Penguin/Random House, 1990), 390.

[23] Peter Senge, The Fifth Discipline, 391.

[24] Peter Senge, The Fifth Discipline, 392.

To give you a sense of how this applies to leadership, I will describe an example of the "limits to growth" archetype I encountered in my own work.

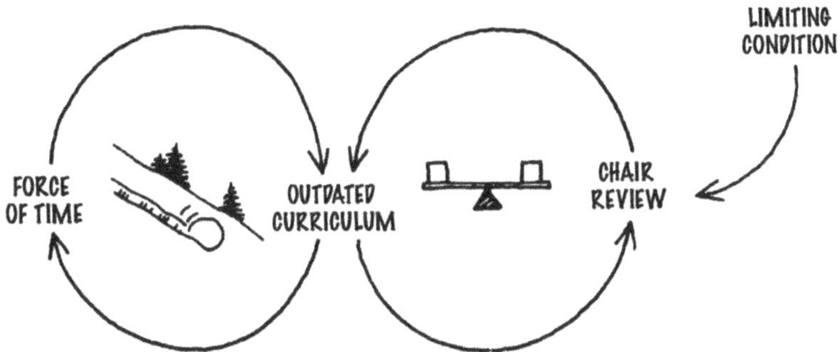

Here is a diagram I generated to help me understand and describe what was happening in my department around delayed curricular updates.

In my department, we are very interested in teaching high-quality, relevant curriculum. This can be hard to maintain – especially in our online courses. They are designed and then delivered as a fixed course shell that is not altered by the faculty who are teaching the course. Established courses require constant updating and improvement, but for years we have struggled to implement a consistent process for course updates.

The left side of the diagram describes the increasing need and urgency of our curriculum to be revised. The snowball indicates the compounding force of time as it pushes our courses out of date, highlighting mistakes that persist from one semester to the next, and causing an increasing number of students to miss out on more relevant content. The right side of the diagram shows the balancing effect on curricular updates by a limiting force. That limiting force is me – the chair of the department, or rather the unrealistic expectation that I must review and approve every curricular change we make to the course shell.

The condition in the middle is the effect of these two forces on our current reality. In this case, despite our urgent need and desire to have highly relevant content in our courses, there were real limits to that growth.

These limits can be understood or shared by sketching out this archetype diagram. With this understanding I was able to describe to faculty (who were feeling an increasing urgency to see curriculum changes) what was slowing down the process. I was also able to work with the online team, our development committee, and our full-time faculty to identify possible solutions.

As a solution, we dispersed some of the review work to our highly qualified, full-time faculty who stepped up to take leadership over the curriculum. Now we have a much quicker approval process and a larger team working on online course development. We have been able to pursue an aggressive development schedule and provide improved content for our students.

The power of systems thinking is found in using simple diagrams to strengthen our creative vision and understand the dynamic forces within a system. Using the same diagrams and archetypes, we can help others see them as well. With new understanding, we are empowered to change the structure and align the forces that will help us overcome the limits to our growth.

CHAPTER 7

NAVIGATE THE CREATIVE JOURNEY

With a clear vision of where you want to go, and an awareness of the aspects of creative vision, your work as a creative leader is to effectively navigate the creative process. The creative process is a series of actions that lead to a novel, imaginative result. These actions are as unique and as varied as the people who enact them. Therefore, this process of translating vision into reality is not a clear-cut, linear, or predictable process. Even calling it a "process" is somewhat misleading. It is, typically, an organic effort that is not proscribed, pre-determined, or understood at the beginning of the creative journey.

While the design process is somewhat linear and more defined, the creative process is ambiguous and fluid. Attempts to organize it into neat stages, steps, or equations ignore the very nature of creativity. Even still, I have noticed consistent elements that can be found in every creative process. I call them the Components of the Creative Process.

I think there is great value – especially for the creative leader – in being able to identify and leverage these so-called components. To help us recognize and remember them, I have divided them into three categories: 1) Action Components, 2) Emotional Components, and 3) Super-Components.

ACTION COMPONENTS

Action Components are things we do in the creative process. Built on core beliefs, these constructive actions bring us closer to the tangible results that we had envisioned for ourselves or our team.

We look forward with an eye of faith and *develop* a strong vision. We *analyze* the discrepancy between our current reality and our vision. We *share* our vision and our creation. We *choose* the best resources to help reach our goals. We *create* with others and close the gap by following through with our vision.

- Develop Vision
- Analyze Current Reality
- Choose Resources
- Create
- Share

Develop Vision

A vast majority of creative processes that produce a meaningful result are previously envisioned. Like sculptors who bring a clear picture of their creation into their minds and then draw it out before pounding the hammer into the stone, we define and articulate the results we seek before jumping into the work. It is important for the creative leader to define the vision in order to lead others to it!

Analyze Current Reality

Comparing our current reality (where we are now) in relation to our goal is an important action step within the creative process. If our objective is clearly defined and we are looking for it, the distance between it and our current reality will become apparent. Just as checking our position with the compass on our way to the harbor will keep us on track, regular comparison will give us a frame of reference for our progress, as long as we are honest about where we are currently.

Choose Resources

As we were reminded in earlier chapters, thinking and acting creatively is a matter of choice. As we sail toward our harbor, we make thousands of decisions that bring us closer to the vision (or further away). We choose how to position our sails, how to use our resources, what knots to tie, when to bring in the sails, and when to shift into the wind. Choosing results and resources in leadership happens when we make vision-based personnel decisions, budget allocations, and investments in the right tools.

Create

It makes sense that if you want a particular result, you have to actually put in work to achieve it. You can choose your harbor, assess your current position, and decide the best way to use precious resources – but then fail to move forward. We might wait, uncertain about our abilities. We might just sit there, never opening the sails. Intentional action leads to creating the results you want. Inaction is still a choice – but will not move you toward your goal.

Share

Engaging in a creative process can be difficult and navigating it on your own makes it even harder. Our creative journeys, challenges, ideas, talents, and results are all meant to be shared. But at times we may hesitate to share the process with others. We might feel apprehensive about sharing our ideas or setbacks. Being honest about the process, willing to share (even vulnerable) is the mark of a creative leader. It will build trust and critical collaboration in our group. Reaching our goals will get easier as we share the load. Like landing our boat on a distant shore, it is important, even critical, to bring others into the struggle to help us land it safely.

EMOTIONAL COMPONENTS

Emotional Components are things that we may feel or experience within the creative process. And it is critical to acknowledge these emotions (whenever they are present) and see them for what they are – *natural indicators of creative momentum.*

- Tension

- Fear

- Ambiguity

- Momentum

- Joy

Tension

Whenever we define a clear vision of our goal, there will be a natural tension between what we want and what we currently have. The tension is uncomfortable. If we don't identify this discrepancy and understand it for what it is, it can quickly overwhelm us or slowly drag us down over time. We might get discouraged and walk away before we reach our destination. How to leverage tension to our advantage is a unique creative skill and explained in the next chapter.

Fear

Fear emerges because risk is inherent to creative endeavors. It is natural to worry about the possibility of failure, our ability to achieve our vision, or what others might think. I am not sure there is any real antidote for feeling some fear – we will feel it often as we create. But hope and persistence will help us move past it. We can also learn to manage risk and overcome fear, or even use these feelings as a motivation instead of a deterrent.

Ambiguity

The creative process is filled with randomness, making it ambiguous (and exciting!). You might be randomly paired with a group of people or have a set of arbitrary resources at your disposal. So, what do we do when things feel messy and ambiguous? Consider this idea from IDEO,[25] a design firm that specializes in leading groups through the design process. They would say: *"Embrace the ambiguity."* If you do that, you may find yourself purposefully injecting randomness into your creative process to encourage novel connections and surprising results.

Momentum

Making progress toward your creative vision can also be fun and exciting. There are moments in the process where stress and troubles drift away and your focus becomes intense. These moments of progress breed momentum, a powerful feeling of energy that is fueled by previous success. Momentum can motivate you to continue translating your vision into reality. It is one of the powerful feelings associated with creating.

[25] I completed a certificate in Creative Leadership with IDEO U – the education arm of the widely recognized design firm called IDEO.

Joy

Joy is more than just feeling good during a creative moment, it is a deep satisfaction that comes from building the results that matter to you. As Robert Fritz wrote, "The reason that you would create anything is because you love it enough to see it exist."[26]

[26] Robert Fritz, The Path of Least Resistance, 59.

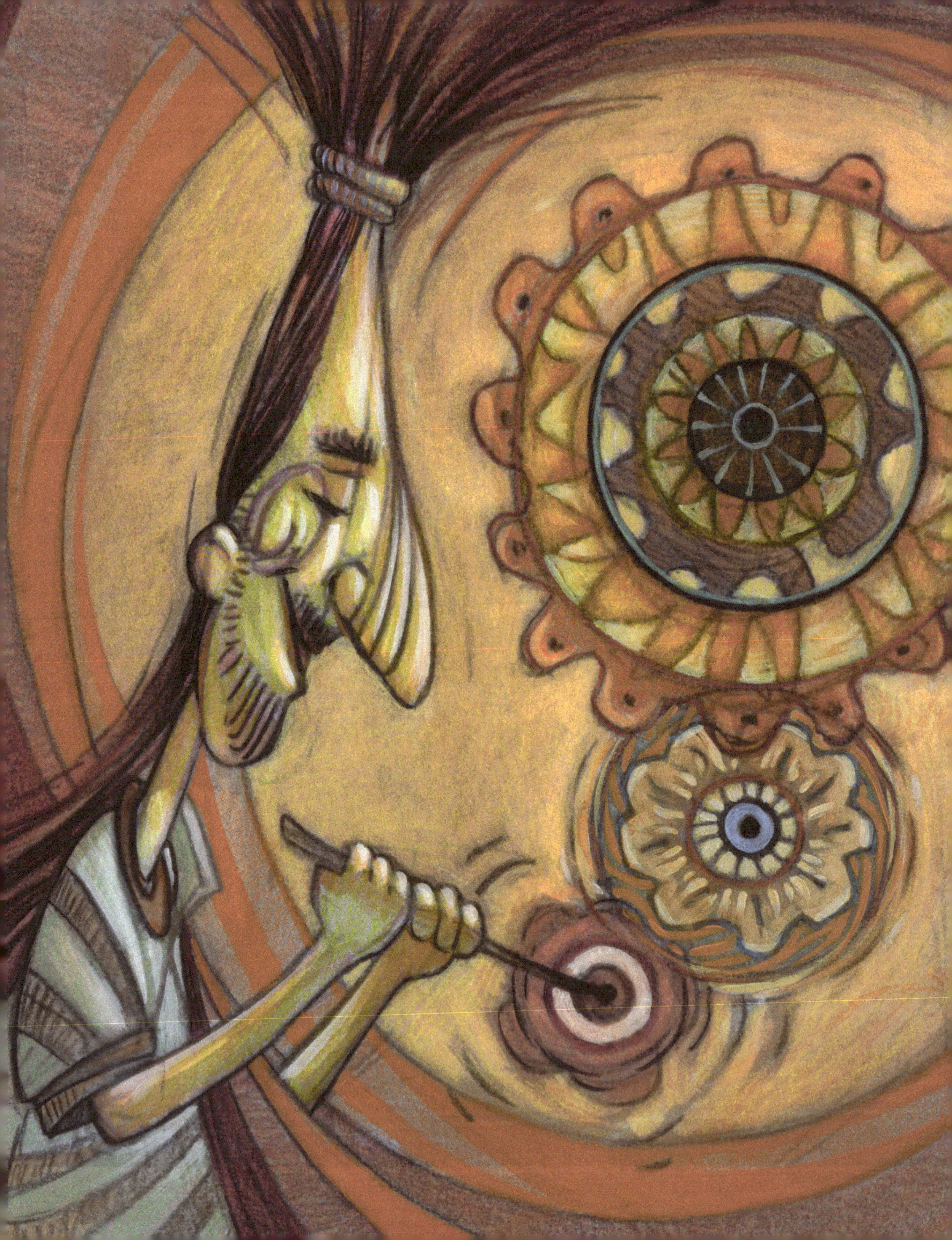

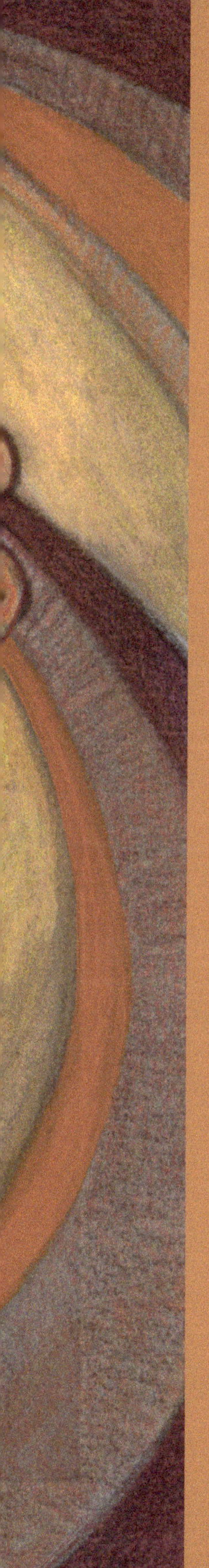

CHAPTER 8

LEVERAGE CREATIVE TENSION

We have identified some actions and emotions that seem to be present (to one degree or another) in every creative process. Action components are task-oriented and are simply things that we do when we are thinking and acting toward creation. We develop, analyze, choose, etc. In the case of emotional components, we can't really dictate the emotions we will have during the creative process. But it is helpful to expect them. It can be extremely valuable to simply identify these components so that you know what you need to do and how you might feel as you build momentum and get closer to your goals.

I would suggest that there are three more components that we should not only identify, but intentionally bring into any creative endeavor. I call these "Super-Components" because they are overarching qualities that will greatly influence our creative results.

These three super-components are conceptual ideals that should be present during the entire creative process:

SUPER-COMPONENTS:

- Imagination

- Collaboration

- Patience

Imagination

We started our discussion of creative leadership with ideas about the imagination. Rightfully so, this is at the fundamental level or beginning of any creative process. But imagination is integral to all parts of the process and should be woven throughout. As a super-component, the imagination should be encouraged and engaged throughout the creative process – especially at strategic points where we need divergent thinking to produce a range of ideas. Imaginative solutions should be encouraged, and there should be room within the process for experimentation and departures.

How do you elevate the imagination in your work and leadership? Do you invite your group to use their imaginative skills? Do you expect experimental ideas from those around you?

The next time you step into a classroom, or ready yourself for work, I want you to remember this question: *"How can I lead with my imagination today?"* If you start every class, every workday, or every project with this question in mind, I think you will see your work in a very different way. This is because imagination helps us to connect the unconnected, bridging the gap between what is and what could be.

Collaboration

Collaboration means that we are working directly with others toward a common goal. This is a super-component because it can greatly maximize our results and effectiveness within any creative process. We can only do so much on our own. Collaboration can be risky and messy but, given the complexity of the issues we face, we need to embrace it.

– Michael Bingham

In a way, collaboration might also mean that we are working with those who have come before us and building on their contributions. When we come to know the people and decisions that have influenced our current reality – it's as if we can become partners with others from the past.

Patience

Above all, patience is the single most important super-component. It is fundamental to other powerful creative attributes such as discipline, persistence, and diligence. More than natural talent, intellect, or any other factor, patience will determine our creative outcomes and results.

Yes, we need knowledge, technical skill, and passion to move a project forward. But we also need a healthy dose of patience with ourselves, with our collaborators, and with the detours along our way. Without patience, most processes fail or stop prematurely, creative ideas never get off the ground, and many people simply give up. Without patience, collaboration stops.

With patience, however, creative leaders are able to take small and simple steps over time to eventually accomplish the vision. They know how to lead others through a creative process that is not linear or bound by a prescribed timeline. They have learned to let the creative process ebb and flow over time. They are willing to patiently move in the direction of their vision, without stressing themselves out by setting unrealistic expectations or arbitrary deadlines.

As a creative leader, it is important to help your team recognize each of these components as they arise throughout the creative process. This is critical because it seems like nearly every creative process has a messy stage, often characterized by fear and ambiguity. As you identify and describe these components, it can help the rest of the team to step back and see them objectively. It illuminates what is happening

– even and especially when it is uncomfortable. When the components become visible, they can be understood and leveraged in positive ways.

CREATIVE TENSION

When I was younger, I played the piano for a few months. Long enough to learn the "Malagueña." It was a simple tune, with a simple structure. It had two repeating phrases, and then a resolution of those phrases – ending with a strong resonant note. My best friend Justin was a piano prodigy. At parties, he would wow everyone with impressive pieces like "The Flight of the Bumblebee." And I was the warm-up act, the foil for my friend's mastery.

If there was a piano, I would sit down and plunk out the "Malagueña." And just to offend my friend's sense of musicianship, I would play the first two phrases and then hold it – keeping the tension in the musical structure unresolved, until he would yell at me, "Resolve! Resolve!" I would finally finish the tune and then yield the piano (and the ladies' attention) to my friend.

Robert Fritz said that in nature (and apparently my friend's musical ear), "Tension seeks resolution."[27] By sensing the tension and leaning into it, we can leverage it to our advantage. But we are not talking about the tension between musical phrases, colleagues, or competing priorities. We are talking about a feeling of discomfort or anxiety caused by a perceived discrepancy between what you have and what you want.

This feeling, that Peter Senge calls "creative tension," is one of the most important reasons for defining your vision in the first place. It is actual-

[27] Robert Fritz, *The Path of Least Resistance*, 76.

ly a good thing! Having a clear objective will set up a tension resolution system that will compel you toward action and resolution.

Senge describes creative tension:

> "People often have great difficulty talking about their visions, even when the visions are clear. Why? Because we are acutely aware of the gaps between our vision and reality... These gaps can make a vision seem unrealistic or fanciful. They can discourage us or make us feel hopeless. But the gap between vision and current reality is also a source of energy.
>
> Imagine a rubber band, stretched between your vision and current reality. When stretched, the rubber band creates tension – representing the tension between vision and current reality... there are only two possible ways for the tension to resolve itself: pull reality toward the vision or pull the vision toward reality."[28]

Do you ever feel a sense of stress when you have a project to complete? As inferred above, that stress will only be eliminated by completing the project or abandoning it. Some people may succumb to this tension and release it by giving up on the vision. They step back from what they truly want. They compromise. Creative leaders, on the other hand, feel the tension and leverage it as motivation and energy to accomplish their vision.

They also learn to position things for their group so that the natural resolution of the tension leads to what they want. With creative vision, they identify the clutter in a system that is preventing their team from resolving the vision. Like clearing the debris out of a ditch so that the

[28] Peter Senge, The Fifth Discipline, 139-140.

water can flow through, they remove the block and provide a natural direction for the process to go.

For me, I seem to translate creative tension into the structure of my calendar. When the project is calling for me to "resolve," I sit down and map out the time it will take and then set up work times on my calendar. In this way, each work session becomes a mini-resolution on my way to completing or resolving the larger project.

Here is a brief example of how I have leveraged tension to close the gap. When I first started my career in speaking and teaching about creative leadership, I decided to give a keynote presentation. Of course, at the time, no one was hiring me to speak about this topic because they had yet to discover its merit. So, I started writing the keynote, rented a large room, and invited a bunch of people. I created my own keynote opportunity!

Why? Well, I wanted to collect and share my ideas. But I also wanted some structural tension. I needed something that would pull me toward my vision of teaching about creative leadership. Inviting people to this event, booking the space, and scheduling a videographer, set up a lot of tension! And I would have to resolve it, one way or another. I would need to practice. I would need to deliver. Ultimately, I resolved the tension by showing up and living my vision.

CHAPTER 9

DESIGN FOR SUCCESS

With the introduction of Systems Thinking in Chapter 6, we moved into our discussion of the strategic level of the creative leadership framework. At this level, creative leaders adopt strategies that will help them make real progress with the groups they lead. This chapter begins our exploration of Design Thinking as a broad mental strategy based on empathy for the end user, considerations related to form/function, and an understanding of design principles and processes.

In practice, design is all about the end user. When we design, we intentionally blend form and function together for the person(s) who will benefit from our design. As a "human-centered approach," the design process starts with researching and understanding what our constituent needs. Then we brainstorm, sketch, and often prototype our ideas. To improve the solution, we use design principles to make our design more pleasing, effective, or user friendly for those who interact with it. In the end, we can measure our success by how well it serves the end user.

To be an effective creative leader, you will need a clear strategy to move your group closer to their collective vision. Design Thinking, with its organized teams and defined projects, can do just that. As you understand and implement design practices, you will move beyond incremental change to accomplish the innovation you seek. And what's great is that the strategies have been clearly defined. If you are looking for a step-by-step approach to reaching your goals – this is it!

Design Process versus. Creative Process
Earlier, you learned that the creative process is an organic effort that leads to a novel, imaginative result. Typically, that effort is not proscribed, pre-determined, or clearly understood at the beginning of the process. In a way, we are navigating a creative journey on our way toward a clear vision, but we may not have a defined path.

Like one segment of our creative journey, the design process fits inside the creative process. It has a clear end point – but that point it is not your destination.

Let's expand this metaphor a little bit. You and your team are taking an extensive trip to a place you have never traveled to before (your vision). You have a very clear idea of where you want to be and when. The entire process of getting there will take planning, timing, good decisions, resources, etc. It will include all the moments of delay, boredom, breathtaking vistas, and the ultimate satisfaction of reaching your destination. Think of this journey as the creative process moving you and your team closer to your vision.

You have a carefully organized travel plan, with maps and itinerary. And you are following a pre-determined route with defined resting points. Your plan includes how many miles you need to go each day. It considers the needs of the people who are taking the journey with you, as well as those you might meet along the way. This part of the creative journey is the design process.

You will notice that it has a beginning, an end, and a defined process in between. It is a predictable creative system that begins with a defined prompt (or problem) and converges around a workable solution.

THE DESIGN PROCESS

While actions vary, there seem to be four broad types of activities within the design process. Just as identifying the components of the creative process is valuable, it is helpful to be aware of these activities within the design process. These activities are: Research, Divergence, Convergence, and Finishing.

- Research

- Divergence

- Convergence

- Finishing

As linear as the design process might be (when compared to the creative process), it would be inaccurate to describe these actions as exclusive stages without any overlap. It is true that research typically occurs toward the beginning and finishing occurs toward the end, but these activities can be repeated throughout the process, and sometimes their order is flexible.

Research:

Often designers speak about design projects or initiatives as design "problems." Perhaps this is because as we come to a design solution it feels like we are solving a problem. If we want to solve the problem we will need a thorough understanding of the problem, including its constraints or parameters. This is where research comes in. At the mention of "research," some of you just had a moment of nostalgic panic – thinking of academic research papers, lots of coffee, and trying to appropriately cite your sources!

Thankfully, we are using the word research to include a broad range of ways to understand the needs of our end user. Simply put, research is information gathering. It might start with a search engine, but should quickly move to interviews, articles, experiential explorations, focus groups, and observation. The designer who takes the time to *fully* understand the problem, has the greatest opportunity to solve it.

Divergence:

200 Gestures. 50 thumbnails. 20 sketches. 5 value studies. 100 Cows.

If you went to art school, this list of preliminary studies might look familiar. Well, maybe not the cows. That came from an assignment where we were asked to visually represent "cow" (or some other assigned word) one hundred times. It was designed to develop our ability to think divergently.

Divergence or Ideation is a critical activity woven through the design process. Divergence means exploring or defining a range of options, ideas, and concepts. And it is not just about changing the form (what the cow looks like); a good designer will also explore the content (is it really a cow?), and the concept (what the cow means), and the context (where the cow exists and how that changes our perception of the cow).

At the beginning of a project, it is common to spend a few minutes brainstorming, arriving at a decent idea, and then moving forward in that direction. But art students are often warned against going with one of their first ideas. They naturally get excited about a solution that they think will work, which might prevent them from *really* exploring other possibilities.

Being able to diverge is not just a good skill for artists, it is necessary for creative leaders. How often do we spend a moment on a problem with our team, and then go with the first solution – or the idea that comes from the loudest person in the room? How often do we allow our students to embrace their first idea – instead of pushing the boundaries of their imagination?

It can be hard to go beyond the early concepts. After you get to the 23rd cow, you hit the edge of the pasture (the proverbial barbed wire fence). You have exhausted all of the common, stereotypical, and easy ideas from the top of your head. Now you have to dig deep!

Convergence:

At some point in the design process, we have to choose an idea or direction and begin to develop it. It is important to converge around a single idea that stands out from the rest. After all, we are trying to solve a problem and one of our ideas might just work! But be careful. There might be pressures that cause us to converge too early. We often have a deadline telling us to "converge now!" We might have a client or a boss waiting for us to converge on an idea and finish the design.

The trick is knowing *when* to leave the rest of the 99 cows standing in the field, and *how* to choose the right one. It gets even more complicated if you are working with other cowboys who have raised and nurtured their best and favorite cow. Naturally, their cow is the best and should be chosen. But only one idea can continue to live. The rest will be sent to the chop house! (Okay, have you had enough of the cow metaphor?)

As creative leaders, we can learn to identify and facilitate convergence within the design process. Convergence is about developing a range of our ideas to the point where we can choose the right direction. It's really about decision making. When we converge, we are moving from a wide range of ideas to a single idea, form, or method for reaching our vision.

Finishing:

"Finishing" is doing the work that brings that single idea to completion or some level of finish. Finishing is not just for the end of the design phase or the end of the entire project, it might happen along the way as various components or stages are finished and ready for the next step. In essence, "finishing" is the design process word for closing the mini-gaps along the way.

LEADERS AS DESIGNERS

To be an effective creative leader, you need to learn to design. This skill will be particularly relevant as you strategically move your team closer to their vision. I am not the first to propose this idea. Toward the end of Peter Senge's book *The Fifth Discipline*, he asks an intriguing question:

"Imagine your organization as a large ocean liner and yourself as the leader, what is your role?" When he asked groups of managers this question, they would often describe themselves as "the captain," "the navigator," or "the helmsman."[29] After some thought, Senge would offer the following:

[29] Peter Senge, The Fifth Discipline, 321.

"While these are legitimate leadership roles, there is another which, in many ways, eclipses them all in importance… The neglected leadership role is that of the designer of the ship. No one has a more sweeping influence on the ship than the designer. What good does it do for the captain to say, 'Turn starboard thirty degrees,' when the designer has built a rudder that will turn only to port, or that takes six hours to turn to starboard? It's fruitless to be the leader of an organization that is poorly designed."[30]

Think about it for a second. What is your role as an academic leader? Do you see yourself as the captain who leads from the bridge? The navigator setting the direction? Or the engineer providing the power? Have you ever considered yourself a designer – designing a system, classroom, or program that leads students to success?

[30] Peter Senge, The Fifth Discipline, 321.

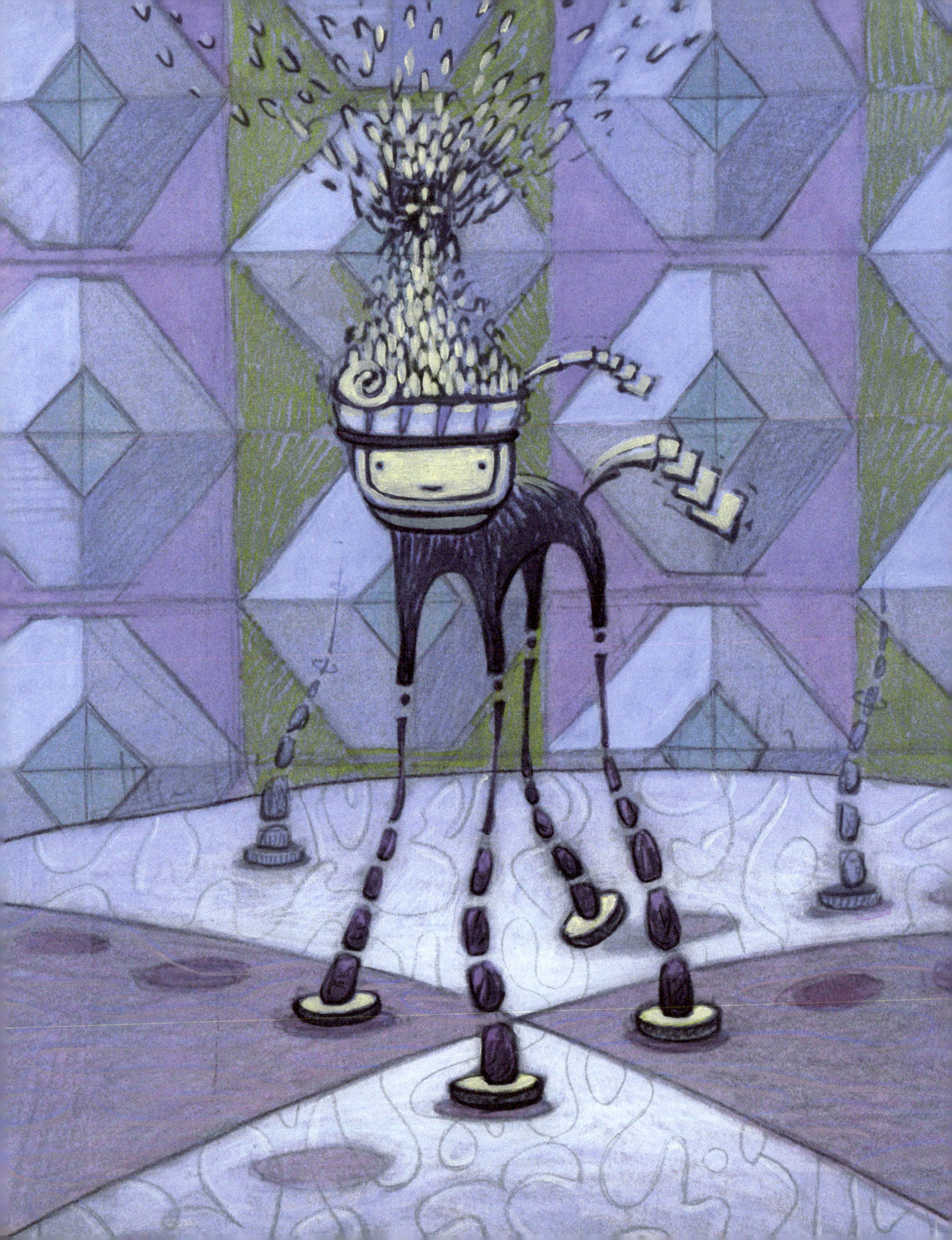

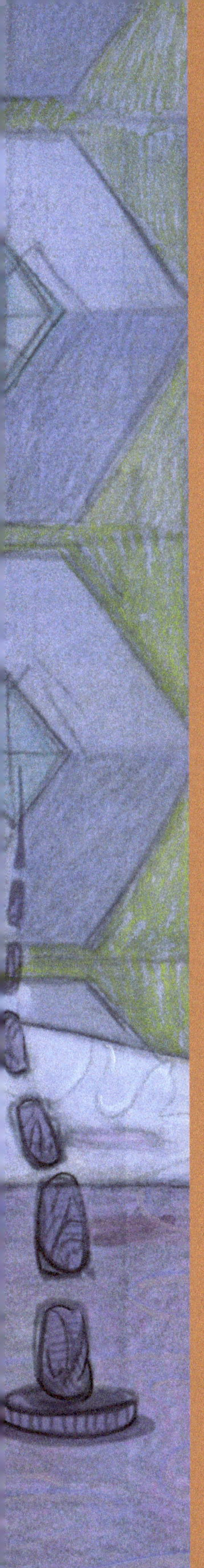

CHAPTER 10

THINK BEYOND INCREMENTAL CHANGE

One way to become a designer is to learn the practice of Design Thinking. In his book *Change by Design*, Tim Brown introduced design thinking as "...a human-centered, creative problem-solving approach [that] offers the promise of new, more effective solutions."[31] He advocates for placing the skills and processes of the designer into "...the hands of people who may have never thought of themselves as designers and apply them to a vastly greater range of problems."

This world needs all types of thinkers and all modes of thinking. We need people who think like scientists, artists, managers, engineers, and musicians. In order to solve some of our hairiest problems, we need people who think like designers.

Tim Brown is the CEO and president of IDEO, a global design and innovation company. As a creative leader, he has made design thinking visible and applicable to business projects. He teaches organizations how to bring the skills of the designer out from "behind the creative walls of the siloed design department and into every part of the organization." Instead of handing the designers a set of "…highly constrained parameters that leaves [them] with little more to do than wrap a more or less attractive shell around a product,"[32] he advocates for putting them on the creative team that considers all aspects of the innovation.

He describes the role of the designer in this way:

> "Design thinking begins with skills designers have learned over many decades in their quest to match human needs with available technical resources within the practical constraints of business. By integrating what is desirable from a human point of view with what is technologically feasible and economically viable, designers have been able to create the products we enjoy today."

– Tim Brown, Change by Design, 10

As a clearly defined process or a pattern of activities that can be followed and repeated, design thinking is a mechanism for innovation that we can employ at strategic points in our broader, creative process. It can be leveraged to accomplish our creative work, collaborate with others, and to create innovative results with our team.

[31] Tim Brown, Change by Design (New York: Harper Business, 2009), 1.

[32] Tim Brown, Change by Design, 29.

Design Thinking is powerful because it is an effective strategy with understandable components that can lead the team toward real innovation – not just incremental improvement. It encourages us to step back and consider how something is designed and then make it better. When we implement design thinking, innovation becomes more than a buzzword or something written in a mission statement – it becomes a reality.

DESIGN THINKING TEAMS

Perhaps an example from academia will help us see how design thinking could be implemented for innovation. Significant investment has been and will be made at nearly every college and university to develop a learning system for online courses. The platform that we use at my institution was first developed about a decade ago. The LMS (as we call it) receives periodic updates and improvements, but the question in my mind is this: *"Will incremental change be enough?"*

Mobile technology and applications have seen tremendous growth and innovation – our platform has not. The current structures and processes limit how much we can do in offering a relevant, diverse curriculum in a format that interacts with today's platforms. How do we avoid the trap of incremental change and truly innovate?

> **DESIGN THINKING IS MORE RELEVANT TODAY THAN IT EVER HAS BEEN. INCREASINGLY, IT'S BECOMING MORE IMPORTANT TO DESIGN AND TO BE AGILE, FLEXIBLE, AND ADAPTABLE.**
>
> – Ad van Berlo

In my mind, we need to invest in a design-thinking project team tasked with developing innovation in this key area of our learning environment.

The Team:

The project team would need to include carefully selected individuals from across the organization. Critical to the forward movement of the project is the ability of each member to think divergently (when appropriate) and then to collaborate with others as we converge around a viable solution. In short, we would need design thinkers with "...capacity and – just as important – the disposition for collaboration across disciplines."[34]

Members of the team would need to represent key constituents at the school, like students and faculty. It would be important to have someone from key groups like academic operations, IT, student services, and instructional design. Lastly, the team would need an appointed leader who has budget authority. A working group or project team is effective because it can bring a group of diverse, interested people together around a common goal. And their efforts can operate outside of the regular maintenance or management of the institution as they explore an innovative solution.

The Project:

Tim Brown explains that a design thinking project is a "...vehicle that carries the idea from concept to reality." Just as a clear vision initiates creative tension, it is the "...clarity, direction, and limits of a well-defined project that are vital to sustaining a high level of creative energy."[35]

[34] Tim Brown, Change by Design, 33.

[35] Tim Brown, Change by Design, 27.

This project-based approach to innovation works well for business be-cause it can have a beginning, end, and defined timeline in between. It allows people to work on the problem in a dedicated way – instead of trying to address the issues sporadically when they happen to get brought up.

The Brief:

A critical component of any design project is how well the leader can describe the problem or opportunity to the team. To get started, they will need a concise description of what is needed. Design thinking models call this the design brief. According to Brown, the project brief is the:

> "...classic starting point of any project. Almost like a scientific hy-pothesis, the brief is a set of mental constraints that gives the project team a framework from which to begin, benchmarks by which they can measure progress, and a set of objectives to be realized."[36]

This brief would need to come from college leadership as it should align with their vision. It would need to be a part of their strategic priorities, plans, and budget. The way that the brief is constructed is critical. Successful briefs concretely describe the result that is desired (the vision), but not the process for getting there. It must be careful-ly crafted and balanced. Too abstract or ambiguous and the project team may be lost or distracted. If the brief is too narrow (or includes a pre-determined solution) the team will be limited to incremental or predictable solutions.[37]

[36] Tim Brown, Change by Design, 28.

[37] Tim Brown, Change by Design, 30.

A good design brief for our LMS project would be:
Within one year, envision, design (or find, leverage, develop), and propose a sustainable platform that offers a comprehensive, interactive system for the delivery of our media-heavy, diverse curriculum. The system should exhibit high levels of interactivity (for students/faculty) and the potential for integration with other student systems (i.e., attendance, registration, etc.). The platform should be designed for the types of learning activities that are critical to student learning in art and design – including demos, critiques, and managing images or portfolios.

The Space:
The project team will need a dedicated, physical space to collect research, document their inspiration, and to come together around a proposed solution. I think about space in both senses of the word, actual and psychological. They will need psychological space (i.e., freedom to work) and encouragement to pursue the best solutions. This is a critical component for success. If we are serious about it, we have to give "space" for it to flourish.

While the project team will benefit from dedicated spaces and resources, they should not feel distant or separate from the rest of the organization. Ideally, they would not be sequestered in their own creative space, but instead become the nuclear part of a pervasive, innovative culture – a culture where everyone understands the vision and comes together at strategic points to give input.

The Process:

With the freedom to work and a clear design brief, the team would begin working through the stages of the design thinking process. This process includes six distinct phases or stages, listed below. You will notice some overlap with the more general activities of the Design Process described above.

1. Empathize

2. Define

3. Ideate

4. Prototype

5. Test

6. Implement

The first two stages involve extensive research as the team works to understand and empathize with the needs of the end user. They schedule conversations, focus groups, and opportunities to observe students using the existing platform. As they keep copious notes and collect experiential information, they continuously refine their understanding and define the problem(s). The next phase is an opportunity to exercise their divergent thinking skills – listing and exploring many possible solutions to address the unmet needs.

[38] Kate Moran, "Design Thinking: StudyGuide" (Nielsen Norman Group, https://www.nngroup.com/articles/design-thinking-study-guide/, 2021).

After a period of convergence that leads them in a feasible direction, the team puts together a prototype (or two) to test the function of their proposals. They will need real users to use it and give them feedback. This helps them test and evaluate the solution. The last phase is to implement – bringing the solution to full resolution. It is important to note that these last three phases may cycle or iterate as more than one version of the prototype might be developed and tested.[38]

CHAPTER II

BALANCE FORM AND FUNCTION

Going through a design thinking strategy like the one just described, would help my institution accomplish our mission of preparing today's students for careers in art and design. However, there is a particular design principle we will need to keep in mind. In addition to knowing how to use design thinking teams, creative leaders need to understand the balance between form and function. If our design solutions are out of balance, we run the risk of irritating and alienating the very people we are striving to serve.

One institution that considered itself a leader in design got lost in the form and forgot the function. The students had asked for a lounge space for resting, socializing, and displaying their creative work. The administration found the investment to support the project and asked the students what features they would like to have in the new space. They hired a design team to translate those ideas into a cutting-edge, student lounge.

Hundreds of thousands of dollars later they presented an award-winning indoor/outdoor pavilion to the student body. It looked like a modern art museum with interactive structural components made of glass and steel. As a work of modern architecture, it was amazing! But it was rarely used by the students.

It was too far away from the cafe to be a viable lunch area. The floor, mini-amphitheater, and tables were all made of cold concrete. The chairs were hard metal. The walls could be used to install art – but then the art was exposed to the elements or vandalism. The TV worked (sometimes), but the remote had to be under lock and key. The space was cold for half of the year. Sadly, it became a running joke for students and a reminder that their tuition dollars were poorly allocated.

What happened? It was clear to the students that the design team prioritized form over function – forgetting to have empathy for the basic physical comfort of the end user. The diagram below helps us understand the relationships between the various concepts associated with form and function. Exploring the form and function balance will help you lead your team through design processes, without losing sight of your end user.

Form gives Significance to the Function

Form and function seem to have a reciprocal relationship. The form gives significance to the function. As an example, think about the basic design and function of a Honda Civic versus a Lamborghini. Both are good cars, but which one stands out? Which one feels significant?

They both have four wheels and get you where you need to go. But people notice vehicles with rare, interesting, or expensive forms. They point out the Ferrari. They stop as you drive by in your Aston Martin. They pause to take a picture with a parked Lamborghini because they like the *form*.

The institution above knew that the form would greatly influence how others received and interacted with the new space. They wanted their student pavilion to be significant, and it was! The design team they hired was known for highly specialized architectural solutions. What they created was the subject of conversations and highly praised for its design excellence.

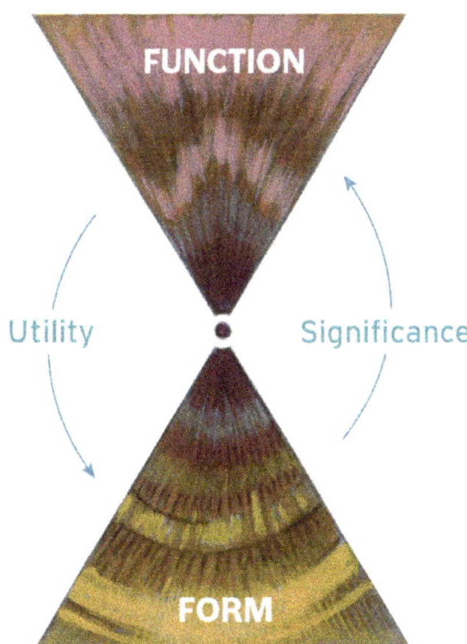

Function gives Utility to the Form

The inverted triangle just above the form triangle in the diagram, represents function. It shows the reciprocal nature of the two. Function makes a design useful. And as stated above, we need both. Your design can only go so far on what it looks like – it needs to work! It needs to solve the problem or provide some benefit or utility to the end user.

To a degree, the student lounge did work. In spite of its steel beams and hard furniture, some utility was offered by the form. It functioned as a

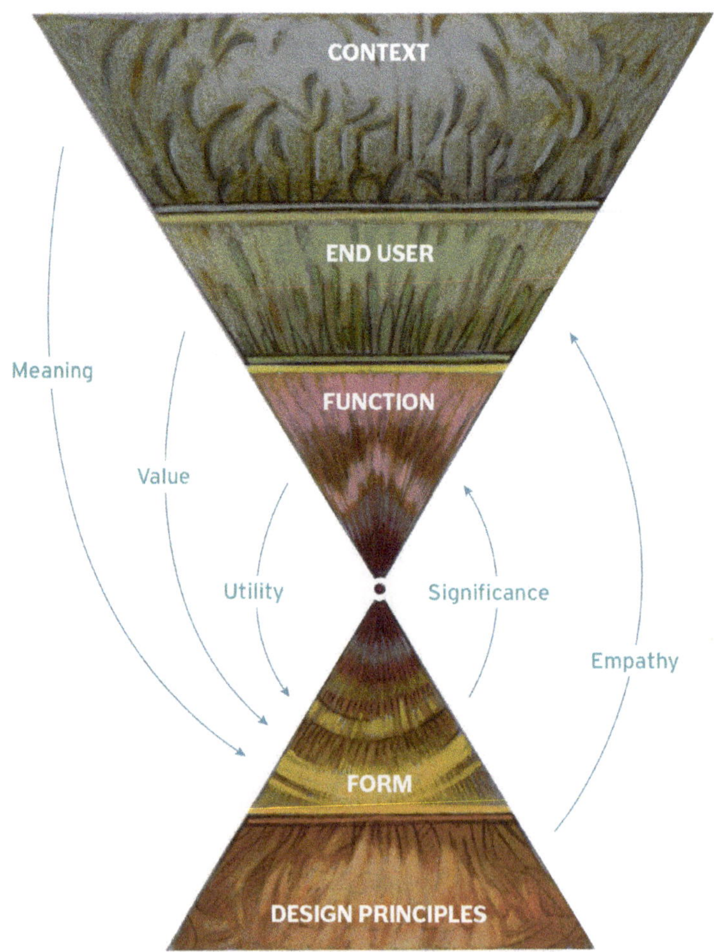

gathering space away from the classroom. Having a lounge was better than not having a lounge. It was cool place to watch the rain or look out over the valley.

Design Principles express Empathy for the End User

Just below "Form" in the model sit the design principles that will be discussed in the next section. Each principle is employed to create a successful design, taking into account the expectations and needs of the end user. In this way, the use of design principles expresses empathy for the needs of the end user. Put another way, you could say that the designer shows empathy or consideration for the end user by their use of design principles.

The concept of empathy must be championed in academic institutions because it is so easy to forget the student end user. How often do we make decisions based on the politics of the situation, what the software can or can't do, or the needs of an external body? How often do we write policies and procedures that are staff-centric instead of student-centered?

End User assigns Value to the Form

Learning this concept changed the way that I thought about my work as an artist. For me, my art was easy to love because, well, I made it! Not only that, I spent a long time on it! But ultimately, it is the end user who assigns value to the form. My mom might assign sentimental value to it and put it on the fridge. An instructor might assign educational value to it and use it in their class. A collector might assign investment value to it and buy it for a million bucks (this hasn't happened yet...). The point is – after I create the form and send it out into the world – I don't get to dictate its value.

Ultimately, the students at the school did assign some value to the pavilion, but certainly not the value that the institution hoped for. That can be a hard pill to swallow, but it will be less painful or even avoidable, if we truly understand this part of the form/function relationship.

Context gives Meaning to the Form

The subject of an art piece is often easy to identify. But the meaning of the subject can be a bit more elusive as it is heavily influenced by the context. Context is the time, place, and space in which the art is created, displayed, and/or interpreted. Context can greatly influence the meaning of the form or the design.

A design that seems ordinary in one context, may be highly valued in another. An example from art history is Duchamp's urinal. Fed up with the art establishment, he pulled a urinal from the men's room, signed it, and submitted it to the gallery as a piece of art. Certainly a ridiculous example, but the *context* changed the way people saw the toilet... and the gallery... and the artist.

The context in which our ideas, programs, words, or creations exist will greatly affect the end user's perception of those ideas, programs, etc. We have seen this many times. A well-meaning group develops a great idea that falls flat (or worse) because they did not consider the context or the factors that would influence public perception.

In the case of the student lounge, the context greatly influenced the student's perception of the building itself. While the institution was watching the walls of their multi-million dollar pavilion get raised, students were watching their tuition go up and well-used classroom equipment deteriorate. In response, students decided to stage demonstrations to protest the tuition increases. Rumor had it that they used the newly constructed student pavilion to meet and make their plans.

PRINCIPLES OF DESIGN

While we may not be able to avoid negative responses in every case, creative leaders can learn to perceive the effect of context and influence the situation for a favorable reception. They can learn to balance form and function as they design solutions with their team.

When working with the design thinking team, it will be critical to incorporate design principles such as Occam's razor, Signal to Noise, and others, into the solution. While considered design principles, these can also be directly applied to your leadership practice.

Occam's Razor

This design principle favors the simplest design solution. Often the simplest design is not easily developed, but leads to the most effective and efficient experience. Complexity in the organization seems to breed complexity into our solutions and initiatives. A creative leader learns to keep it simple, favoring the simple solution over the convoluted.

Signal-to-Noise Ratio

Designers (and leaders) should be careful with the amount of "noise" in a design that distracts or obscures the signal or message. Like the crackling static in a radio signal, sometimes our best attempts to enhance an idea just end up adding noise and making communication more difficult.

Framing

In art and design, the use of a "frame" enhances meaning and eliminates distractions. Conceptually, it can help direct the eye, elevate the work's importance, and help us show others what we need them to see. Framing (in leadership) helps us to communicate and provide valuable context for initiatives and conversations. Creative leaders learn how to carefully frame each problem, discussion, or request, directing others to what is most important.

SUMMARY:

We have explored the distinction between the creative process and the design process. If the creative process is the long journey leading to our envisioned destination, and the design process is one segment of that journey, then the design thinking project is the "...vehicle that carries the idea from concept to reality."[39]

This powerful vehicle can be customized to drive your group closer to meaningful change and innovation. It becomes part of an intentional culture of innovation that is critical within our large academic organizations – where many in leadership seem to yearn for some sense of control in the face of uncertainty and complexity. Their desires come to the surface as conservative decision making, rigid policies, overbearing procedures, and one-size-fits-all approaches.

Without creative leaders who make space for innovation, limited growth and incremental change is the result. Without design thinking as a mechanism for problem-solving and reaching our vision, the real needs of our students may never be met.

[39] Tim Brown, Change by Design, 27.

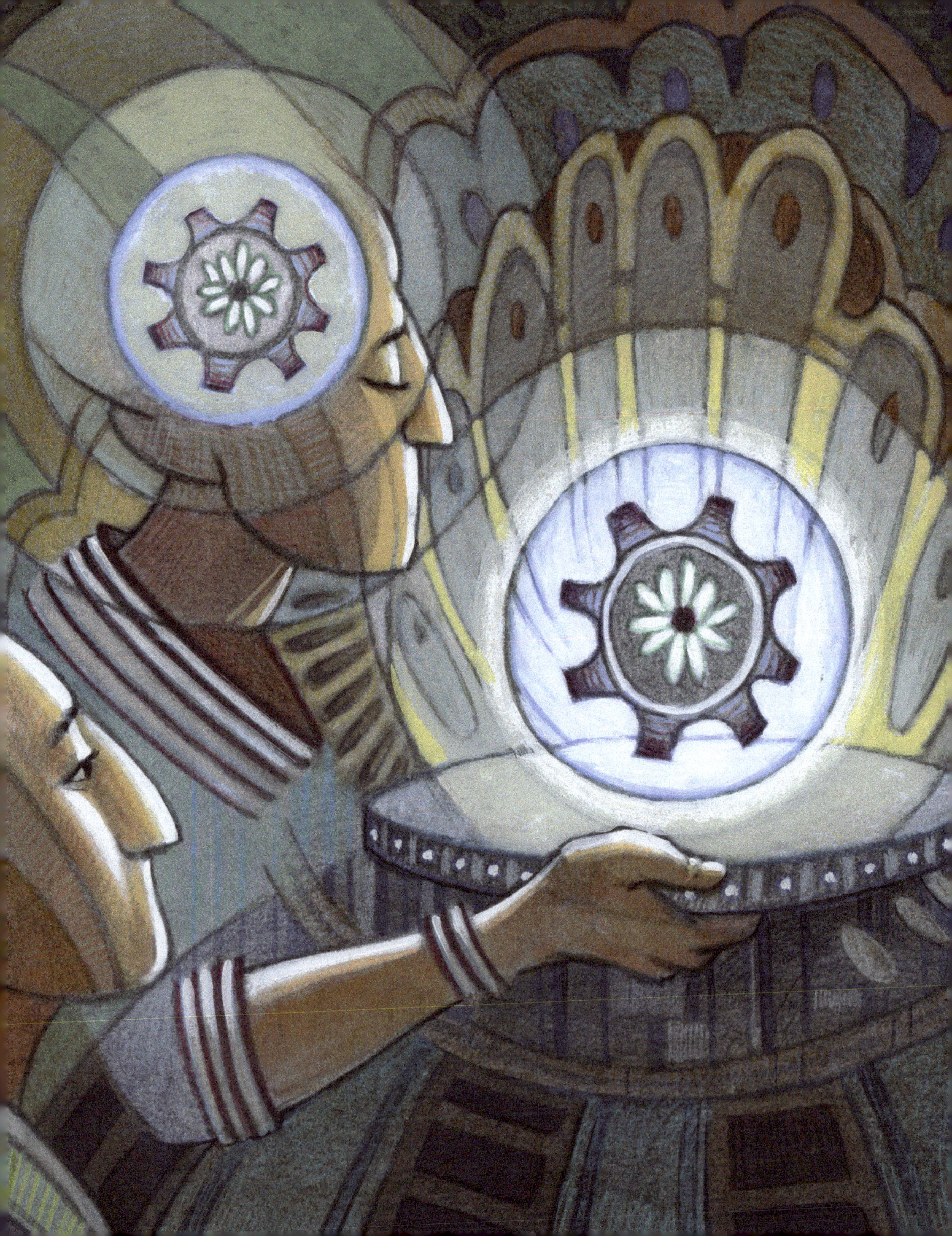

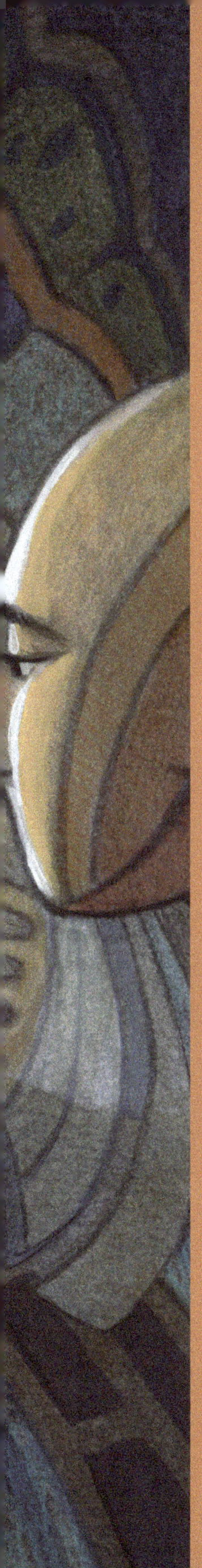

CHAPTER 12

MAKE YOUR THINKING VISIBLE

Your team is gathered around the conference table, laptops open, discussing the latest trend, challenge, or initiative. Like many other strategy meetings, the leader presents the topic and tells you what they think about it. One or two questions are posed (to the leader) and then a couple of ideas are tentatively floated from members of the group. After each suggestion, the group turns to the leader and waits to see their reaction to the idea. If he or she likes an idea, the discussion might continue toward possible action items. If not, the group throws out more ideas or moves on to other topics. Fairly typical, yes?

Now instead imagine a meeting focused around a large whiteboard or "canvas" where the leader has posed a question and mapped out the latest trend, challenge, or initiative. You are handed a set of sticky notes and a marker. Someone sets a timer and the group now has three minutes to propose solutions to the question at hand. You jot down some ideas and place them on the canvas.

Everyone stands back and can see the ideas laid out on the canvas. The leader begins to discuss each idea in turn and then organizes the ideas into groups of similar solutions. After some discussion, the group begins to gravitate toward a solution with the most potential. The leader sketches out some of the key components of the solution and outlines some preliminary action items.

There are various differences in each scenario but, to begin with, simply consider these two questions: What is the committee seeing? What do you notice about their focus?

In the first scenario, they look to the leader to validate each idea. They are likely somewhat distracted by looking at their laptop or the spreadsheet that they were working on. They cannot see the challenge that is being discussed, but they can feel the power in the room.

In the second scenario they are looking at the canvas together. They see a visual representation of the challenge. This makes an abstract challenge visible, leading to better communication and further engagement. They see ideas of equal size and weight – which removes the politics from the room and allows the best idea to surface.

Which type of meeting would you actually *want* to attend? In my experience, these types of active, visual discussions are rarely used – except for maybe at the annual retreat. The rest of the year we default to meetings without much visual thinking.

Visual Thinking will take many forms or modes. But basically, it is the process of giving visual form to abstract ideas. It may look like sticky notes on a whiteboard, charts, diagrams, or large drawings. And it can be very powerful strategy, especially when applied to leadership and group collaboration. This is because once an idea has been formed (even if it is just a sketch), it can then be seen, interpreted, analyzed, and more importantly – added upon. Visual Thinking can help our team find better solutions and accomplish our vision.

Creative leaders see the value of visual thinking and strive to make their thinking visible for group members. To do this, they follow a pattern of seeing, drawing, and sharing. In this context, the idea of "drawing" should not be interpreted too narrowly. Some leaders may get intimidated when they think about drawing, but we are not talking about highly-refined artistic masterpieces here. More broadly, the creative leader's definition of drawing includes any possible way to make your thinking *visible*.

One of those ways is prototyping. A prototype is a quick, low-tech way to give form to an idea so that you can test it. This will help you close the gap. When your ideas become tangible you can, as Dan Roam explained, develop "…ideas quickly and intuitively, and then share those ideas with other people in a way they simply 'get.'"[40]

[40] Dan Roam, quoted by van der Pijl, Lokitz, Solomon, Design a Better Business (Hoboken: Wiley & Sons, 2016), 173.

There are huge collective benefits to sharing your "drawing" as a way to collaborate and get on the same page with your group.

Additionally, there are positive personal benefits as well. Here are a few that Willemien Brand describes in her book Visual Thinking.

"WHEN YOU DRAW…

- You order your thoughts.

- Patterns and links become clear.

- It simplifies.

- You get new ideas.

- It opens people up.

- People stop focusing on small, irrelevant details.

- It makes the subject approachable."[41]

[41] Willemien Brand, Visual Thinking (Amsterdam: Buro BRAND and BIS Publishers, 2017), 13.

In our creative leadership framework, the strategic level is where we intentionally choose the types of thinking strategies that will be most appropriate for the work we need to accomplish. We might need to implement design thinking, systems thinking, or visual thinking – or some combination of the three to achieve our vision.

You could say that these three thinking strategies or disciplines are all inherently visual – and that would be correct. But visual thinking has its own set of tools and skills that can be infused into your leadership activities. It will be important to discuss it as a distinct strategy and learn to employ the tools, skills, or modes of visual thinking.

LEARN TO SEE!

This is not a drawing book, but we will use some ideas or concepts from the act of drawing to explain visual thinking, beginning with the concept of learning to see. The activities of seeing and drawing are highly integrated with one another.

As a drawing instructor, you could say that I have spent my career teaching students how to draw. But I would say, I have been teaching them how to *"see."* This is because with observational drawing you have to learn to see (and understand) what you are drawing, before you can describe it accurately in your drawing.

Two common seeing errors prevent students from learning to draw well. First, they fail to truly *observe* the subject because they think that they already know what it looks like. Instead of an accurate depiction, they end up drawing a simplified or symbolic version of the subject as they default to their own ideas or concepts of what is in front of them. With this error, they are drawing symbols of things – a symbol of an eye, instead of the unique eye of the person they are drawing. They draw a symbol of the bottle, instead of representing the unique proportions of the unique bottle in front of them.

This is like leaders who fail to truly observe the needs of their constituents or group members, because they think they already know what those needs are. Then they offer a generic, symbolic solution that may not be what that group needs.

– Patrick van der Pijl

Students should spend more time looking at, studying, or observing their subject than they do working on their drawing. My drawing instructor often said, "Draw what you know, not what you think you see."[42] To really draw something well, you must *know* your subject. It is best to understand it from every angle and to even know what is on the inside. Perhaps this is one reason that artists try to understand the skeletal structures and muscle groups of the human body. What we see on the surface is simply an outward manifestation of what is on the inside; the structure of the muscles, bones, and fat under the skin. If we only draw what we can see, without an understanding of what we know, our drawings are one dimensional and uninformed.

Like an artist studying human anatomy, creative leaders study their current reality intensely. They understand that what they can observe at the surface level of an organization, individual, or problem is simply an outward manifestation of their inner structures, beliefs, or systems. They know that they need to look beyond the symptoms on the surface, imagine the structure, and reveal the causes. This clear understanding of the problem helps them "draw it out" and explain it to others.

[42] Leon Parson, Professor at Ricks College.

Secondly, art students often lose sight of overall relationships, i.e., how things relate to one another within the subject or the composition.

The act of drawing forces you to look carefully at what you are drawing. But focusing too intensely on one part of the subject can cause you to lose track of how it relates to the other elements. Students get irritated when they spend time studying and drawing the model's hand, getting it just right. And then they step back and see that the arm is too long or at the wrong angle. In order to get their drawing right, they would have to redraw the hand that they just drew. Usually, they don't.

To avoid this myopia in leadership, creative leaders learn to *step back* during the design process and see the whole, instead of just their part of the project, problem, or organization. They expand their creative vision and maintain a clear sense of the big picture. (see Chapter 6)

Beyond learning to clearly see the subject at hand, learning to draw is about accurately representing the *relationships* that we see. Various relationships exist within the subject, such as shape, color, value, scale, angle relationships, and so forth. If the artist can recreate those same relationships in their drawing, they will have an accurate drawing. The challenge is that all of those relationships are simultaneously and constantly affecting each other within the artwork. If one part is too dark (as it relates to everything else), that part will simultaneously make everything else appear lighter than it really is.

Creative leaders know that understanding and representing relationships accurately is critical. They see relationships in the landscape of their life and work. They work hard to understand those relationships as the people near them constantly change and relate to each other in different ways.

LEARN TO DRAW!

In my drawing classes I use an acronym to help students learn to draw from observation. I often set up a still life of simple forms like bottles and cans or cardboard boxes for them to draw. Sounds easy right? How hard can it be to draw a stack of cardboard boxes? Try it sometime and you may be surprised by the challenges you encounter. This list will help you remember and see the relationships in what you are drawing.

SEE THE RELATIONSHIPS:

- **P = Parallel Lines:** two forms that are parallel to each other

- **I = Intersections:** where two lines meet

- **A = Alignments:** an imaginary line helps us see an alignment between two forms

- **N = Negative Space:** the background or the space around the object

- **O = Overlaps:** one object overlapping another

- **S = Scale:** the relative size comparison between two objects

If you can see these relationships in the subject, you are more likely to represent them accurately in the drawing.

So, how does this tie into Creative Leadership? As you know, part of the work of a creative leader is to help others see. We can help them to see connections, relationships, patterns, systems, forces, etc., in their workplace, classroom, or at home. We can help others see where groups might intersect, how they overlap with one another, or how they align. Using simple visual language, a creative leader helps others see how two elements of the organization are working in parallel.

P = Parallel Lines

Greater unity within a drawing is developed when there are some forms or lines that are parallel to each other. When they share that characteristic or orientation, they seem to relate to each other in a unified way. In a similar way, when two groups or individuals are working in tandem and moving in the same direction there is greater unity, strength, and momentum on the project.

I = Intersections

Whenever two lines meet, or objects overlap in a drawing, you can identify an intersection. Accurately placing that intersection helps the artist to place the objects into the right visual relationship. When you are working with various groups, it is important to strategically place some intersections – meetings, check-ins, conversations – into the workflow or timeline. Accurately placed intersections will help the groups make connections and understand their relationship to each other as they work together.

A = Alignments

Even in an average sized drawing, distance can be a problem. Sometimes an object on one side of the composition will be hard to place accurately because it is far away from other objects or reference points. Its relationship with other elements is hard to see. Have you ever seen an artist close one eye, extend their arm in front of themselves, and hold up a pencil or a short stick? They are looking for alignments. Holding a stick horizontally (or vertically) so that it is visually touching one form allows them to see how that form relates to something on the other side of the composition.

In our hybrid working environments, distance can be a problem. Creative leaders find ways to see and describe the alignments between various groups on the other side of the organization. Helping their team see the bigger picture will help them connect and collaborate with those who are not "just down the hall."

N = Negative Space
Negative space is the white space or blank space around an object. In drawing you can draw the positive space (the object), or you can shift your paradigm to see and to draw the negative space (what's around it). This actually helps you to see the object more accurately. With some challenges or problems, it is easy to focus too intently on the problem itself. The solution might be found by stepping back and thinking about the space or environment surrounding the challenge.

O = Overlaps
When one object overlaps another in a drawing, we usually understand that to mean that that object is in front of the other one in space. This helps to establish depth or a sense of hierarchy in the composition. An overlap will also obscure our view of the other objects behind it. An overlap in our project or working space might mean that two efforts are redundant and should be consolidated. Or that one effort is being obscured by something else and we cannot see the full picture. It can be helpful to look for these overlaps and draw them out for your team.

S = Scale

Scale means relative size. Like age or other relative qualifiers, something is not "big" unless there is something smaller to compare it to. In a drawing, the size of one thing can be determined or established by comparing it to the size of something else. Artists manipulate or exaggerate scale all the time to tell the story. They make the antagonist large on the page and overbearing when compared to the smaller protagonist.

As we are striving to navigate the endless stream of information and ideas coming into view, it seems like every idea, project, or constituency demands equal attention or has equal weight. Using visual thinking strategies and tools, a creative leader can learn to describe the scale of a concept when compared to something else. This will help our team or our students know where to put their energy and focus.

Look for other connections between your work (or life) and the PIANOS acronym for drawing. You can learn to see problems, structures, and priorities as you give them form and make them visible. This will also help you as you try to help others see. Identifying and then describing the parallels, intersections, alignments, and negative spaces will help everyone see fundamentally important relationships.

CHAPTER 13

SHARE WITH MODES OF VISUAL THINKING

Words are critical, but pictures, stories, and visuals will bring color and clarity to your message. There are various methods or techniques to accomplish this – too many to count, list, or describe. But I will describe what I call the Modes of Visual Thinking. A mode is a distinct way that we can utilize visual thinking in our classroom or leadership role. These modes are broader than any particular technique. In fact, they are composed of many methods, techniques, and/or activities that move teams through various stages of the design process.

Each visual thinking mode is designed for a particular purpose as described below.

Using the modes of visual thinking, we can solve one fundamental problem that limits our effectiveness when doing imaginative work. In their book called The Imagination Machine, Martin Reeves and Jack Fuller describe this challenge as the "problem of intersubjectivity."

"How can two private mental worlds align to work together on the same mental 'object'? This is less of a problem when you're dealing with things that already exist. If you show something in the real world to your neighbor, you can point to it and say, 'Let's talk about that.' But if you are in the middle of imagining something, it doesn't yet exist. Especially if you want to share imagination with someone while the idea is still nascent and amorphous."[43]

[43] Reeves, Fuller, The Imagination Machine (Boston: Harvard Business Review Press, 2021), 93.

Using simple words, I call this the "I can't read your mind" problem. Reeves and Fuller go on to suggest improved communication as the solution. They propose being intentional about how we name things, use stories, listen, focus, and work or play together. All of these are true and important. However, like many organizations, teams, and classrooms, they are missing an opportunity to enhance communication with the tools and techniques of visual thinking.

Their book is an excellent resource for understanding the imagination and how we can create "collective imagination and momentum to turn ideas into new realities."[44] But their answer to the problem of sharing imagination is missing one important piece – the modes of visual thinking. We have to find a way to sketch abstract ideas and make them visible!

Under each of the modes below, I will include an example of visual thinking techniques that you can use to improve intergroup communication during imaginative work. I won't go into detail about each technique or give proper instructions. I am simply sharing an example and referring you to other resources for the specifics.

Vision Forming

The more clarity you have about your vision, the easier it will be to know when you have achieved it. This is a surprisingly simple concept that many of us forget. Instead of a clear vision, we develop a lazy, hazy idea for what we want, and then spend a lot of time and energy working toward an ambiguous end result. Instead, we should spend more time and energy forming our vision and getting really clear about what we want. It is hard to overestimate the importance of using images, sketches, prototypes, or drawings to form your vision.

[44] Reeves, Fuller, The Imagination Machine, 6.

Ideation

Simple drawings, paired with one or two words, are an excellent way to capture ideas when you are diverging with your team. Instead of only using words in your next brainstorming session, require group members to draw their ideas as well. Your group will achieve greater communication, engagement, and clarity, as they explore each idea.

[45] Willemien Brand, Visual Thinking, 77.

[46] Sarah Stein Greenberg, Creative Acts for Curious People (New York: Ten Speed Press, 2021), 173.

Facilitation

When you need to do some planning with your team or explore some undeveloped ideas with your students, you can use visual thinking techniques to facilitate that process. Don't ignore the importance of your visual format. Formal slide presentations are nice, but because of their polished format they feel finished or complete – even if the idea is not. This will limit the imagination, feedback, and the willingness of group members to explore the idea. Using rough drawings or other objects to facilitate planning or learning can be very effective and much more efficient at early stages of your process.

Storytelling

A huge part of our communication is accomplished by telling stories. With a story you can engage your listener's senses and they will remember your point. For even greater effectiveness, learn to tell your story with pictures. Even simple drawings will help your team or students to remember your main ideas, concepts, or proposals.

Describing Systems and Structures

Creative leaders use drawings, symbols, shapes, and directional arrows to effectively describe the patterns, forces, or relationships in a particular system. When we speak of a system, we are normally speaking about the *dynamic* aspects of the context in which we live and work. The forces or pressures seem to constantly change or evolve. Structure, on the other hand, is more rigid. The structures are the constraints, parameters, policies, and organizational charts that provide a framework within which we have to work.

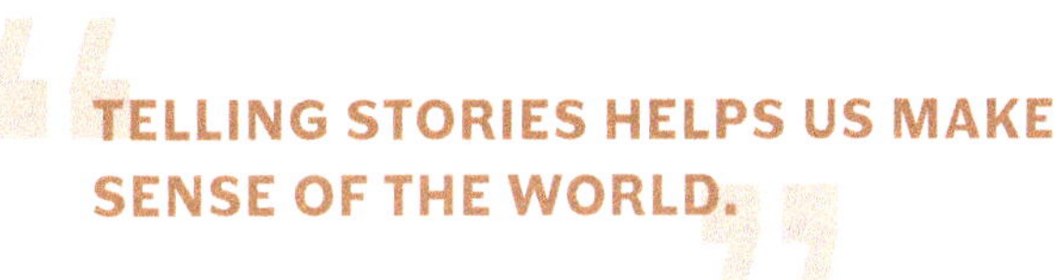

– Willemien Brand

Structure is not the same as a system. Systems are fluid, structure is rigid. My daughter is very fast at jigsaw puzzles. I puzzled with her one day and discovered why. She didn't just look at the image printed on the puzzle piece and then try to match it to the overall image, she also noted the shape of each piece. Did you know that while each piece has a unique part of the image on it, the shape of it is not unique? If you study the edges (the structure) of each piece,

47 Willemien Brand, Visual Thinking, 53.

you will see repeated common shapes. And those repeated shapes interlock together in predictable ways. She was faster because she could see the structure of the puzzle, not just the image on the surface.

Sometimes we are simply unaware of the structures that we are operating within. Or we don't fully understand the system or the dynamic forces at play. Creative leaders diagram the system until they truly understand it. They engage their imagination and drawing skills to envision it until they can describe it. They describe it with models, images, diagrams, stick people, whatever!

VISUAL THINKING TOOLS

The other day I had to step in and sub a class on linear perspective. The classroom had a large monitor for presentations, an overhead document camera, a tablet for digital drawing demos – and no dry-erase marker. I thought, *"How can anyone teach in this room without a marker!?"* I had to steal one from another classroom. A marker is a simple, but critical tool for visual thinking.

[48] Sarah Stein Greenberg, Creative Acts for Curious People, 247.

As you may have noticed, you don't need any fancy software to utilize visual thinking techniques. In fact, the tools are very simple. In van der Pijl's book on designing a better business, the word "canvas" is used to denote the paper, board, or other large space where visual ideas are seen and discussed. Sticky notes are good because they are easy to place and move. Their size limits the concepts to a few words – this will help to distill the idea during the ideation sessions. Obviously, you need something to write with. Dark permanent markers work well on paper. A variety of colors may help add interest.

PRINCIPLES OF VISUAL COMMUNICATION

Within every design are certain elements, such as shape, color, value, time, texture, or line, etc. Over time, artists and designers have learned that there are more pleasing or effective ways to compose these elements to convey form and meaning. The most effective ways have become guiding principles that influence the use, arrangement, or manipulation of the elements. Of course, each of these principles are informed by empathy for the viewer or the end user.

We find principles of composition and design in paintings, illustrations, sculpture, product designs, music, films, and a host of other areas where something has been designed or composed. For our purposes, we will briefly introduce a handful of principles that have application to leading groups through creative processes with visual thinking.

As a creative leader, looking for effective ways to make your thinking visible, you only need to remember three broad principles. The principles of Hierarchy, Rhythm, and Unity encompass a wide subset of smaller concepts that artists and designers use in visual communication. They are explained here to help you evaluate the visual design and effectiveness of your communication. If other people are misunderstanding your diagrams or pictures there might be a more effective way to arrange visual elements.

Establish Hierarchy

Within a design, it is helpful to create a hierarchy. This means that some elements, ideas, or functions are treated differently to convey their importance. Those elements become dominant within the composition and other elements will become subordinate. We control hierarchy on our canvas so that some things stand out. We might make the title bigger so that it is read first, or add colorful, bold outlines to certain words to emphasize their importance.

Create Rhythm

One of my professors used to say, "Same, same, same is boring, boring, boring." That was usually in response to a student who had unintentionally created a very regular pattern of elements within their work. This regularity made the work less interesting, even boring.

Rhythm is created by the repetition of elements and the space between those elements within our visual design. When you engage your team with repetitive visual elements, remember to create interesting rhythm. Vary the space or distance between words, objects, or images.

We can also think of rhythm as it affects our workflow. Have you attended a regular weekly meeting with the same group for years? Changing up the regularity might spark some irregular ideas.

Increase Unity

It seems to be in our very nature to categorize things and identify those things that are the same. Our brains seem to group similar elements together and we feel pleased when there is unity within a design, a group, or a project. Visual thinkers use grouping, repetition, and placement to show how some concepts are connected or related to other ideas.

SUMMARY:

Beyond the tools and techniques we have discussed in this chapter, there is one key point that needs to be emphasized. You can learn to get better at drawing by using symbols or working with visual metaphors. You can learn to make your thinking visible to others. It doesn't matter what mode or tool you use. The tools and techniques will likely change with each situation anyway; but if you can show people your thinking, you will find greater success. They will be able to give you well-informed feedback. They will be able to see where you are headed and will want to follow you. You will have greater clarity in your own mind as you envision, draw, and share your ideas with words, stories, and pictures.

EXPANSIVE ACTIONS

This section describes creativity at the synthesis level as the fusion of all creative beliefs, thoughts, and expansive actions that creative leaders combine as they lead others toward accomplishing their vision. We describe the power of metaphor, the gifts of effective teaching, and how to create a culture of innovation. In the end, leaders are invited to lead with their imagination, acknowledge the messy stage, and to maximize the creative efforts and abilities of individuals and teams – helping them translate their vision into reality.

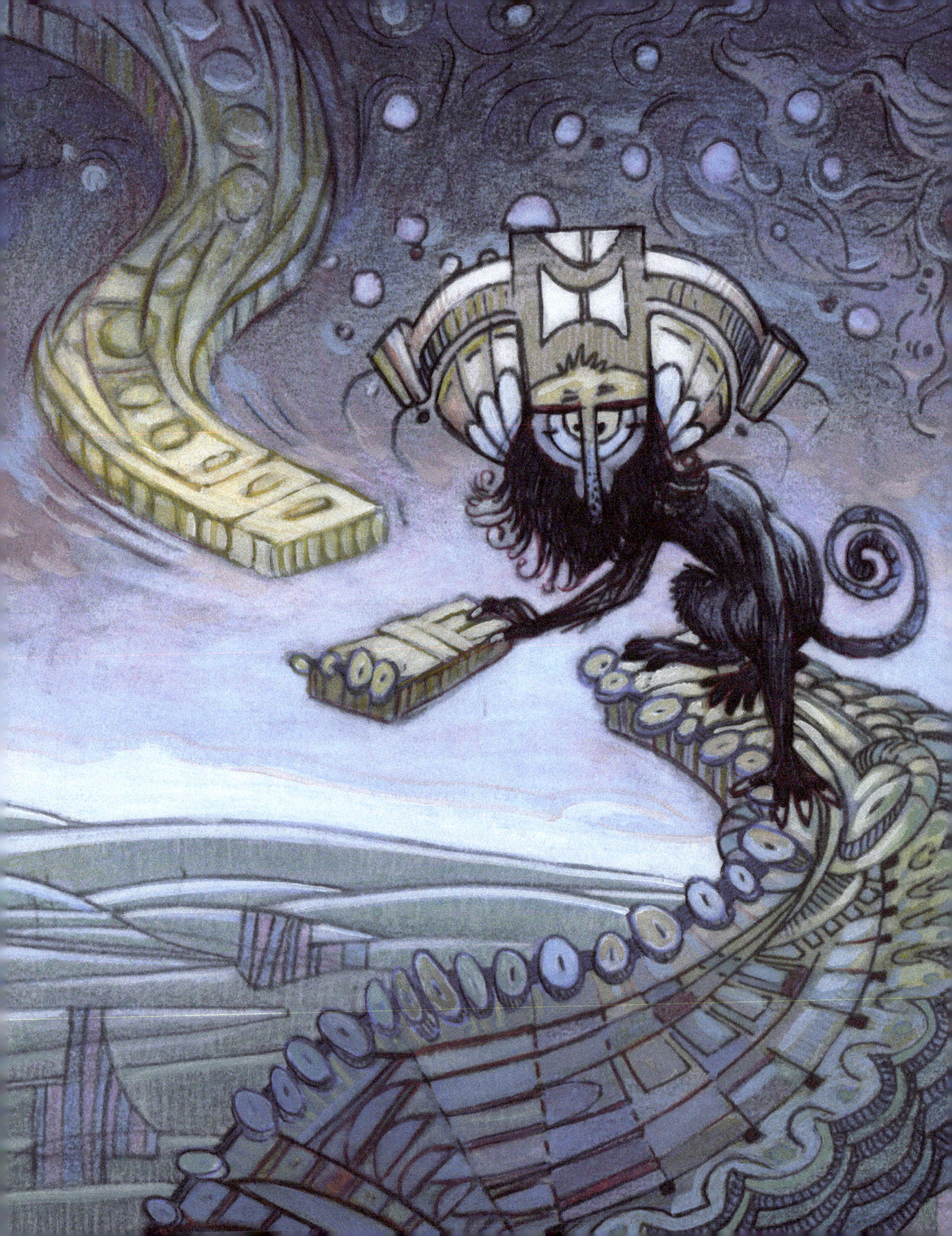

CHAPTER 14

CLOSE THE GAP

With a clearly defined vision in place and an understanding of the elements within the creative process, the work of a creative leader is to lead their team in closing the gap. This is the stage where we synthesize our thinking strategies and actions into accomplishing the vision. This work requires us to leverage creative tension, make vision-based choices, and learn to manage the emotional components of the process.

"WE CHOOSE TO GO TO THE MOON...!"

One of the most distinct examples of creative leadership was launched in Rice Stadium, Houston, Texas, on September 12, 1962, and came to fruition in July of 1969. John F. Kennedy, the 35th president of the United States, described his plans (his vision!) for putting an astronaut on the moon.

Before describing a clear vision, Kennedy offered his audience a glimpse of the context in which it existed at that time. He detailed the sharp and dramatic increase in learning and technological advance that was happening in the 20th century and how it related to the scope of human history.

Then he described certain values (noble ideals) that were motivating him and his team.

> "For the eyes of the world now look into space, to the moon and to the planets beyond, and we have vowed that we shall not see it governed by a hostile flag of conquest, but by a banner of freedom and peace. We have vowed that we shall not see space filled with weapons of mass destruction, but with instruments of knowledge and understanding.
>
> ...In short, our leadership in science and in industry, our hopes for peace and security, our obligations to ourselves as well as others, all require us to make this effort, to solve these mysteries, to solve them for the good of all men, and to become the world's leading space-faring nation."[49]

[49] John F. Kennedy, We choose to go to the Moon! speech (Houston: Rice Stadium, September 12, 1962), paragraphs 10-11.

The description of his goals and the reasons behind them provided a moral foundation which gave strength and power to his ambitious vision. Kennedy continued his speech, getting very specific about the next steps. His vision was so clear that it inspired an entire nation.

> "But if I were to say, my fellow citizens, that we shall send to the moon, 240,000 miles away from the control station in Houston, a giant rocket more than 300 feet tall, the length of this football field, made of new metal alloys, some of which have not yet been invented, capable of standing heat and stresses several times more than have ever been experienced, fitted together with a precision better than the finest watch, carrying all the equipment needed for propulsion, guidance, control, communications, food and survival, on an untried mission, to an unknown celestial body, and then return it safely to earth, re-entering the atmosphere at speeds of over 25,000 miles per hour, causing heat about half that of the temperature of the sun – almost as hot as it is here today – and do all this, and do it right, and do it first before this decade is out – then we must be bold."[50]

He knew that this was a bold vision. And one that would attract the attention of the naysayers and the skeptics. In a sense, he was setting up tension that the whole nation could feel. Here is what he had to say to them:

> "But why, some say, the moon? Why choose this as our goal? And they may well ask why climb the highest mountain? Why, 35 years ago, fly the Atlantic? Why does Rice play Texas?

[50] John F. Kennedy, We choose to go to the Moon! speech, paragraphs 23-24.

> "We *choose* to go to the moon. We *choose* to go to the moon in this decade and do the other things, not because they are easy, but because they are hard, because that goal will serve to organize and measure the best of our energies and skills, because that challenge is one that we are willing to accept, one we are unwilling to postpone, and one which we intend to win, and the others, too." *(emphasis added)*

Here is a short list of the ways that John F. Kennedy demonstrated creative leadership in this instance. You will likely see even more.

KENNEDY'S CREATIVE LEADERSHIP:

1. He could clearly see and was able to describe the forces, structures, and systems that we would be dealing with. He was using systems thinking.

2. He could see with the eye of faith "new metal alloys" and other technologies not yet invented.

3. He used great detail to describe the resources that would need to be developed and chosen.

4. In essence, he developed a clear "design brief" for those whom he was leading, one that was so clear it carried us through to completion after his tragic death.

5. He demonstrated deep confidence in the abilities of those around him. Even while laying out this plan, he clearly acknowledged the potential he could see in the people who would be working toward this great project.

[51] John F. Kennedy, We choose to go to the Moon! speech, paragraphs 13-14.

Evidence for the credibility of this leadership style is the fact that we actually closed the gap – even after he was gone. Seven years and 240 thousand miles is a pretty big gap! But we did it because of his vision and leadership. His success was based on the strategies and principles of creative leadership.

MAKE EFFECTIVE CHOICES

I love Kennedy's use of the word "choose." Because a huge part of closing the gap and creating the results that matter to us is how we use our power to choose. Maybe this goes without saying, but we are constantly making decisions that will affect our results.

Making effective choices a crucial aspect of closing the gap and realizing your vision. An effective choice will move you and your team closer to your vision. You will find that not every choice will be effective – but when it is not, you will have the opportunity to learn what doesn't work and you can make a different choice. The key is to continue using your agency to make choices, instead of allowing other things to make the choice for you.

As an art teacher, I hear students say something like: *"I don't have my homework because..."* And usually, it has nothing to do with their dog or any factors that are truly outside of their control. More often than not they describe how the printer didn't work, how they got called into work, how they ran out of time, or how they didn't have the right tools, the right paint, etc., etc.

That is what they say... but what I hear is this: *"I am unprepared be-cause of bad planning and less-effective choices."* More specifically... I hear: "I *chose* not to maintain the printer, or buy ink, or go to a print shop, or stop by campus to use the printer. I *chose* to go into work. I *chose* not to stay up late after work, or wake up early to get my work done. I *chose* other priorities instead of my homework. I *chose* to not have the right tools or find the right paint."

Over time, they get better at planning and making choices and they become less affected by their circumstances. Thankfully, this can be the case for each of us! In his book *The Path of Least Resistance,* Robert Fritz describes several ways we unintentionally fail to make effective choices:[52]

1. **Choice by limitation:** choosing only what seems possible or reasonable

2. **Choice by indirectness:** choosing the process instead of the result

3. **Choice by elimination:** eliminating all other possibilities so that only one choice remains

4. **Choice by default:** the "choice" to not make a choice

5. **Conditional choice:** imposing external preconditions on your choice (I will do this, if this happens...)

6. **Choice by reaction:** choices designed to overcome a conflict

7. **Choice by consensus:** choosing by finding out what everyone else wants

8. **Choice by adverse possession:** choice based on a "hazy meta-physical notion about the nature of the universe"

[52] Robert Fritz, The Path of Lease Resistence, 167-171 paraphrased.

In each of the scenarios above, we are allowing something else to dictate our choices and this is an indication of a reactive mindset. Creative leaders cannot afford to abdicate their power of choice to outside forces. They cannot step aside and let circumstance dictate their decisions.

Now, we may not always be the decision maker in every situation. Sometimes we have to accept that someone else is leading and we must follow their direction. But for everything that *is* under our control, we should strive to make effective choices.

So how do we do that? If there are so many ways that we can fail to make effective choices, how do we implement a creative mindset and make them more productively?

- Choose results that matter
- Choose your vision over circumstance
- Choose the process
- Choose resources and tools

Choose results that matter (to you!)

It is clear from his speech that Kennedy had developed a clear vision and had studied current reality. He knew where we were at and what it was going to take to get to the moon. But it is also clear to me that before outlining the plan for how this could happen, he had clearly chosen the result. Out of all the other priorities, he was choosing to get us to the moon!

How often do we choose results that matter to someone else like our spouse, our boss, or our staff? This is tricky, because what we want can sometimes conflict with the goals of these other parties. What do we do then? If we can't explain this and resolve it with them – we have to find a way to own it, to intentionally choose it – choose it as a result that really does matter to you. If the result matters to you, you will have passion for the work to get it done. And you will have integrity and congruence, instead of compromise.

Choose your vision over circumstance (develop courage!)
Circumstance is a force that we must choose to overcome, not just once, but all the time. Like an untrained puppy, circumstance has a way of constantly reminding you of just how many interruptions, messes, and complications stand between you and your desired outcome. It gets discouraging, disappointing, and painful.

With patience and persistence, continue to choose your vision over your circumstance. You might need to adjust methods and strategies along the way, but don't lose sight of your vision.

Choose the Process (or system for success!)
Meaningful results come about through a process of creation. It is not by happenstance – it is by design. In addition to choosing a clear vision, we have to choose and design the process that leads us there. So, what is process? Process is a set of steps or actions that are intended to lead us to our goal. You could think of it as a system that will activate component parts and move us forward.

Adam Morgan, Executive Creative Director at Adobe, explained this concept in an article called: "How I Wrote My First Book By Avoiding

Goals." He described ten years of setting a goal to write a book at the beginning of the year, and never finishing it. He even asked his friend to hold an envelope with a $100 bill until the end of the year. If he finished his book, he got his money back. If not, his friend got to keep it. Even that was not enough motivation.

Turns out, he didn't need motivation. He needed a system.

> "Everyone makes goals, but successful entrepreneurs do something very different. They create systems… that continue to work, every day, regardless of any goals.
>
> I looked at my goal of writing a novel and thought seriously about what system I would need to create to succeed. I created a writing group with other authors who also wanted to finally write a book or screenplay. We set aside Thursday nights right after work as the time. We would meet at a neighborhood clubhouse that was always quiet and had a few tables and couches. We would set a timer for an hour. Write. Take a ten-minute break. Then set another timer for an hour. That's it. All you had to do was show up… I didn't have to think about it or set aside time to write. I just showed up every Thursday night at the clubhouse at 7 p.m. and wrote for two hours.
>
> And here's the best part. After only five to six months, three of us in the group finished writing a book. The day I finished writing my first book I was thrilled. I had actually done it. The guilt of the past decade was gone. Along with the worries that maybe I wasn't cut out to be a real author."[53]

[53] Adam Morgan, "How I Wrote My First Book By Avoiding Goals" (https://medium.com/the-creative-machine/how-i-wrote-my-first-book-by-avoiding-goals-7c21b1b2082c).

Choose resources and tools (invest in success!)

You can have amazing, creative ideas but choosing and using your resources wisely is critical to your success. Being able to close the gap comes down to choosing the right resources and the right tools. Tools don't have to be fancy – but they have to fit the need. They need to work.

When I was younger, I enjoyed the game of golf. As a teenager with a summer job, I was somehow able to afford it. As you may know, golfers have different types of clubs to do different things. There are drivers for long distance, wedges to escape difficult areas, and short-range putters to carefully push the ball into the hole. Some of my friends played an entire round with a putter because they didn't have the proper clubs or didn't want to carry the bag around the entire course.

Needless to say, that was less effective. But it is not much different for some of us at work or school. Many of us seem to choose the same type of club (or tool) – regardless of the challenge at hand. Instead of taking time to carefully design or find the tool that will be most effective, we choose the tool that we are comfortable with. It is true that sometimes, we just have to work with what we have. But in many cases, the best creative solution is to find the right tools and the right people to accomplish the project.

By choosing the right tools, and the most effective systems, we can position those we lead for success. It takes great courage to choose vision over our circumstances. But if we have also chosen results that matter to us and develop courage, we will be investing in their success.

CHAPTER 15

ACT DESPITE UNCERTAINTY

Earlier, the great creative leadership of John F. Kennedy was described. His presidential approach was impressive! But what if you and I aren't leading an entire nation into a new era of space travel? What if our objectives are much more terrestrial – just trying to manage the chaos of life and work? Can we still demonstrate creative leadership and learn to close the gap? Of course!

In fact, our youth might even be some of the best examples of creative leadership because they seem to treasure and use their imagination, leading others in the process.

As an example, let's see what we can learn from the life of Homer Hickam. He was a young boy with limited resources who found a way to accomplish his vision and launch himself beyond very difficult circumstances into a college education, a career as a NASA engineer, and on to become a very successful writer. His memoir Rocket Boys became a #1 New York Times best-seller. (I guess we are keeping with the space theme).

We will explore anecdotes from his life that align with Four Action Steps for Closing the Gap. These principles highlight the aspect of working to close the gap. There is no substitute for hard, sustained, prioritized work. As alluded to earlier, results that matter don't just happen, they are created as we put in the work.

FOUR ACTION STEPS:

- Develop Resources

- Act Despite Uncertainty

- Test with Prototypes

- Calibrate Constantly

After witnessing Sputnik streak across the sky in 1957, Homer (Sonny) became fascinated by the "whole thing" and was determined to learn how to make and fly a rocket. This became his vision and the accompanying tension became a driving force behind his learning and growth. As a coal miner's son, he was destined to be a miner. But learning to make rockets changed the course of his life. In spite of his lack of support and resources, he found a way to accomplish his vision and became a creative leader – closing the gap on his vision with his team, the BCMA (Big Creek Missile Agency).

Develop Resources

The resources you need to close the gap are not just money or more staff, it might mean reorganizing or reappropriating the resources you do have. As a leader, you might need to learn to say "no" to some things, so you can say "yes" to the important things – and move valuable resources to those projects that move you toward your vision.

A big challenge for Sonny and his friends was a significant lack of resources. They didn't have a lot of money. And even if they did, it wasn't like they could just order a rocket kit. They had to create their rockets from the ground up. As they worked toward their objectives, they gained valuable knowledge and resources – sometimes at the expense of their family.

> One morning, Dad plunked bread slices in the old toaster that sat on the counter and pushed the mechanism down and then went to the stove to pour coffee. When he came back, the handle on the toaster was still down, but nothing was happening. He discovered the heating element was gone, mainly because I had taken it to see if my plans for an electrical-ignition system would work.[54]

At one point they needed some tin to build a small mission control building and discovered that the Reverend had just gathered a little stack of tin to repair the roof of the church.

O'Dell told him what we needed. "Love to help ya, I really would," he said, "but I don't have enough for my roof as it is."

I looked up. "But your roof is shingled."

He nodded. "If I had shingles, I'd use 'em. But I don't. I've got tin." "Emmett Jones has a bunch of shingles stacked up next to his coal box," O'Dell said. "Almost the same color."

"Do tell," Little Richard said, suddenly interested. "I reckon I'd be up for a swap if you could manage it."

We were starting to learn how to trade, Coalwood-style. We found Mrs. Jones pushing a lawn mower. "Emmett's at work," she said, "but if you'll bring me a load of good plantin' dirt, those old shingles are yours."[55]

After a couple of hours of "picking and shoveling rich, black West Virginia loam into the truck," they delivered the dirt, retrieved the shingles, and traded for the tin. Success!

Developing resources, however, is more than just finding tools, equipment, or software. It also includes developing knowledge, skills, and abilities. Creative leaders embrace a growth mindset and learn what they need to know.

Previously considered to be a poor algebra student, Sonny wanted to learn trigonometry so he could...

[54] Homer H. Hickam, Jr., Rocket Boys (Dell Publishing, 1998), 146.

[55] Homer H. Hickam, Jr., Rocket Boys, 117.

"...figure out how high our rockets were flying. I delved into Jake's book. Quentin, delighted to have it, did the same. Sitting together in the Big Creek auditorium at lunch, we taught ourselves trigonometry. I had discovered that learning something, no matter how complex, wasn't hard when I had a reason to want to know it."[56]

Act Despite Uncertainty

In nearly every creative endeavor, there is an element of risk or uncertainty. Success favors those who act, move forward, and build creative momentum. For Sonny, it was a struggle to find the best rocket fuel to push his rockets into the sky.

"First, we mixed up several small batches of what we hoped was black powder and, as a test, opened the grate and threw a spoonful of each into the coal-fired hot-water heater beside the washing machine. The ingredients hissed feebly... "What do you think?" I asked. Quentin shrugged. Neither of us knew how rocket fuel was supposed to burn."[57]

Later, they discovered a highly volatile solution – something they called "rocket candy" – made with saltpeter and sugar. But they realized that they would need to melt it (very slowly) before it was loaded into the rocket. Sonny was unsure.

For the first time since we began building our rockets, I hesitated. "I don't know, boys," I said. "That sounds like a prescription for getting our heads blown off." The others stood around me, looking concerned and thoughtful...

[56] Homer H. Hickam, Jr., Rocket Boys, 134.

[57] Homer H. Hickam, Jr., Rocket Boys, 117.

"What do you think, Quentin?" I asked.

Quentin shrugged. "This one's your call, Sonny. It is a step into the unknown, I'll warrant, but... It would be a fantastic propellant, I'm sure of it!"[58]

Notice the cloud of uncertainty in the room as his team waited for him to make the call. As a creative leader with a clear vision, he was the one who would need to act in spite of the uncertainty. It turned out to be a "fantastic propellant" and launched their rockets hundreds of feet into the sky. Like Sonny, creative leaders move forward into the unknown with hope and resilience.

Test with Prototypes

All too often we have a meeting, develop a plan, and move directly into implementation without testing the plan. Prototyping or versioning is an excellent way for a creative team to learn what works (and what doesn't) before committing all of our valuable resources. Sonny's missile agency was an excellent example of using prototypes. Some of their early attempts didn't go so well.

"Flames burst from *Auk II*. It sat for a moment, spewing smoke and sparks and rocking on its fins. Then it jumped ten feet into the air, turned and zipped into the woods behind us, ricocheted off an oak tree, rebounded back to the slack, twisted around once, twanged into the boulder Quentin and I were hiding behind, jerked twenty feet into the air, coughed once, and dropped like a dead bird.[59]

Sonny quickly learned that failure was not necessarily a bad thing or something to be embarrassed about. Creative leaders learn this, too –

[58] Homer H. Hickam, Jr., Rocket Boys, 156.

being willing to test, fail, experiment, prototype, and learn from their supposed mistakes.

> "Without Quentin, I might have been too embarrassed to fail in front of God and everybody. With him, no matter what happened, I felt 'scientific.' Failure, after all, just added to our body of knowledge."[60]

Calibrate Constantly

Every decision we make will either move us closer to our vision or further away. That is not meant to stress us out, but to develop the habit of considering how each choice will ultimately lead us to (or away from) our vision. To calibrate means to consistently evaluate where you are in relation to your vision, and then make necessary adjustments to get closer to your goal.

After a series of smaller test rockets, Sonny and his team went from *Auk I* to *AUK XIV*, a rocket that reached three thousand feet! Finding just one quote to make this point is difficult, since his entire book is basically a series of calibrations that eventually led to astonishing results. They adjusted for different types of fuels, encasement materials, construction methods, weather conditions, designs, and rocket sizes, etc. As a creative leader, his vision and patience for constant calibration was remarkable.

[59] Homer H. Hickam, Jr., Rocket Boys, 91.

[60] Homer H. Hickam, Jr., Rocket Boys, 71.

MANAGING EMOTIONAL COMPONENTS

In Chapter 7, you were introduced to the components of the creative process. If you recall, there are three types of components – action, emotional, and super. Emotional components in particular, are often present when we are trying to close the gap. They are feelings, ideas, or concepts that seem to be inherent in the creative process. As you work toward your vision, it is helpful to identify and acknowledge these feelings with your team so that they know what is happening and can effectively manage them.

Embrace the ambiguity

In the chapter on creativity, we described four distinct manifestations of an individual's imagination. They are: 1) artistic expression, 2) making stuff, 3) problem solving, and 4) innovation. While we are bound to feel some uncertainty in each category, there seems to be higher levels of ambiguity with innovation.

The stakes are higher, and the risk of failure is greater, since we are working toward something novel or previously unknown. Innovation also involves the imaginative and constructive skill of synthesizing each aspect of our imagination to reach our vision. Logically, the greater the unknown and the higher the level of synthesis required, the greater the ambiguity.

But creators have learned to manage ambiguity, even embrace it.

One simple example of innovation (and ambiguity) from my experience was when I created a picture book for kids called Woodchuck

Chuck. I am sure you have heard the woodchuck poem that goes like this:

How much wood could a woodchuck chuck,
if a woodchuck could chuck wood?
He would chuck all the wood that a woodchuck could,
if a woodchuck could chuck wood.

When I was younger, my dad used to tell me silly stories and poems, including this tongue-twister about the woodchuck. He could say it *really* fast! It wasn't until I was a dad that I could say it really fast too! When I was still in school, I met an editor who liked my work and wanted to know if I had any stories I was working on. I told him about my dad, and the woodchuck poem. We started brainstorming and came up with a character named Woodchuck Chuck.

I turned to my friend Rich McDermott who had a talent for writing to write the story. We worked on draft after draft, and I made hundreds of sketches. Over the course of about three years, I sent multiple versions of the woodchuck story to the editor. (Some of them were pretty bad!)

For some reason he continued to work with us. Finally, I felt like we had a great version of the story. It had become the story of a little woodchuck who could not go chuck wood with his dad because he was too little. Instead, he ended up chucking Quick Quack Duck, Big Pig Ben, and the little Red Hen high into the air. With confidence, I sent it to the editor and waited… and waited… and waited… I never heard back.

So, after about four years of sitting in that reactive mindset, I decided to self-publish. That decision became a clear vision – I wanted to see the book exist. But it also increased the creative tension and ambiguity about how exactly that would happen.

The great thing was that I had complete creative control over the final product. The problem was... that I had complete creative control and had to do it all! There were plenty of things that I had never done before. I had to figure out the artistic style of the book, do each painting, find an editor, design the layout, and discover the process for printing, shipping, marketing, distribution, sales, etc. There was plenty of ambiguity!

Even though I felt lost at times and unsure if my plans would work, I embraced the ambiguity and patiently worked through each moment of uncertainty. That is what embracing the ambiguity means – not getting overwhelmed when you don't have the answers.

It means choosing to hold the vision and see it through to resolution in spite of the unknowns. In time, I was able to translate my vision into reality. With the book in hand, I was able to visit elementary schools and hold assemblies for the kids. Together we would read the story, make up new stories, do scribble challenges, and explore other ways to inspire creativity.

The constant presence of ambiguity breeds a necessity for patience within the creative process. Without patience with the process, the messiness, the randomness, the ambiguity – creative work comes to a halt. And it is not just creative projects or lack of innovative solutions at work that are affected; it can be long term success in life that is at risk without patience.

You should know that patience is not reactive, i.e., sitting back and waiting for the circumstances to change in your favor. No, patience is refusing to give in or give up – diligently working to change the situation and to do what we can in spite of the circumstances.

Fear in the "Ugly Phase"

As with other creative endeavors, artists experience a range of emotions in the process of making a painting. There are moments of joy, but also uncertainty and fear that can creep in and set us back. There are parallels to leadership here that if understood, will help you navigate the uncertainty of the creative process.

Before adding details to my paintings, I almost always experience a moment in the process that I call the ugly phase. This is where I step back and look at the unfinished image or face – and it looks like an abstract mess of brushstrokes. At that point, I feel very uncertain about the outcome. I have found that the only way to move forward is to withhold judgment and keep working. Over time, the painting comes closer and closer to my vision.

The same thing can happen in leadership. The objective that was once so clear, seems impossible now when compared to your current reality. Fear takes hold when you suddenly see your work objectively and it is clearly miles away from what you had envisioned. Your team feels the momentum slipping away.

> Uncertainty on the way to our vision happens when our well-laid plans get lost in the messiness of the initial creative process. The only way to move forward is to withhold judgment and keep working. Over time and with patience, we will get closer and closer to our desired destination.

And it can be particularly difficult when other people randomly insert themselves into the project or process you are trying to lead. They might pop into the process with judgment – pointing out the abstract messiness of the ugly phase. They might not have a clear vision of where you are going or want to see the details prematurely.

Being able to manage your emotions, acknowledge the ugly phase, and clearly describe where the group is at in the process will help you navigate these moments. Inexperienced leaders will tend to panic or stop in the middle of that messy creative tension. But a practiced creative leader will continue to work and to wait, knowing that with enough practice and active patience, the vision will emerge from the messiness.

Understanding this natural part of the process will help the group continue with patience and faith. Leaders who don't understand this aspect of the creative process will struggle to help their group work through it. They will fail to leverage the tension and close the gap – leaving their team stranded in the discomfort of discrepancy.

"Happy Accidents"

As challenging as the ugly phase may be, there are also moments that artists call "happy accidents." Of course, we like to think that every stroke, every movement is intentional and produces the intended result. But sometimes, the paint moves a certain way that was unintentional – and actually turns out better than we had designed. It was accidental, but it makes us happy!

As you create and work toward your vision, it is important to remain open and flexible about the process. Don't judge yourself or the product too harshly, especially in the middle of the project. Acknowledge the emotions and the messiness. Refuse to get caught up in ideas about failure, or having to control everything. Instead, allow unexpected events, happy accidents, and randomness to help you reach your destination.

Just like John F. Kennedy, we can define a bold vision and make vision-based (effective) choices. Like Sonny, we can learn how to calibrate constantly, test with prototypes, and learn from our experiences. In both cases, these two creative leaders managed to embrace the ambiguity and act in the face of great uncertainty.

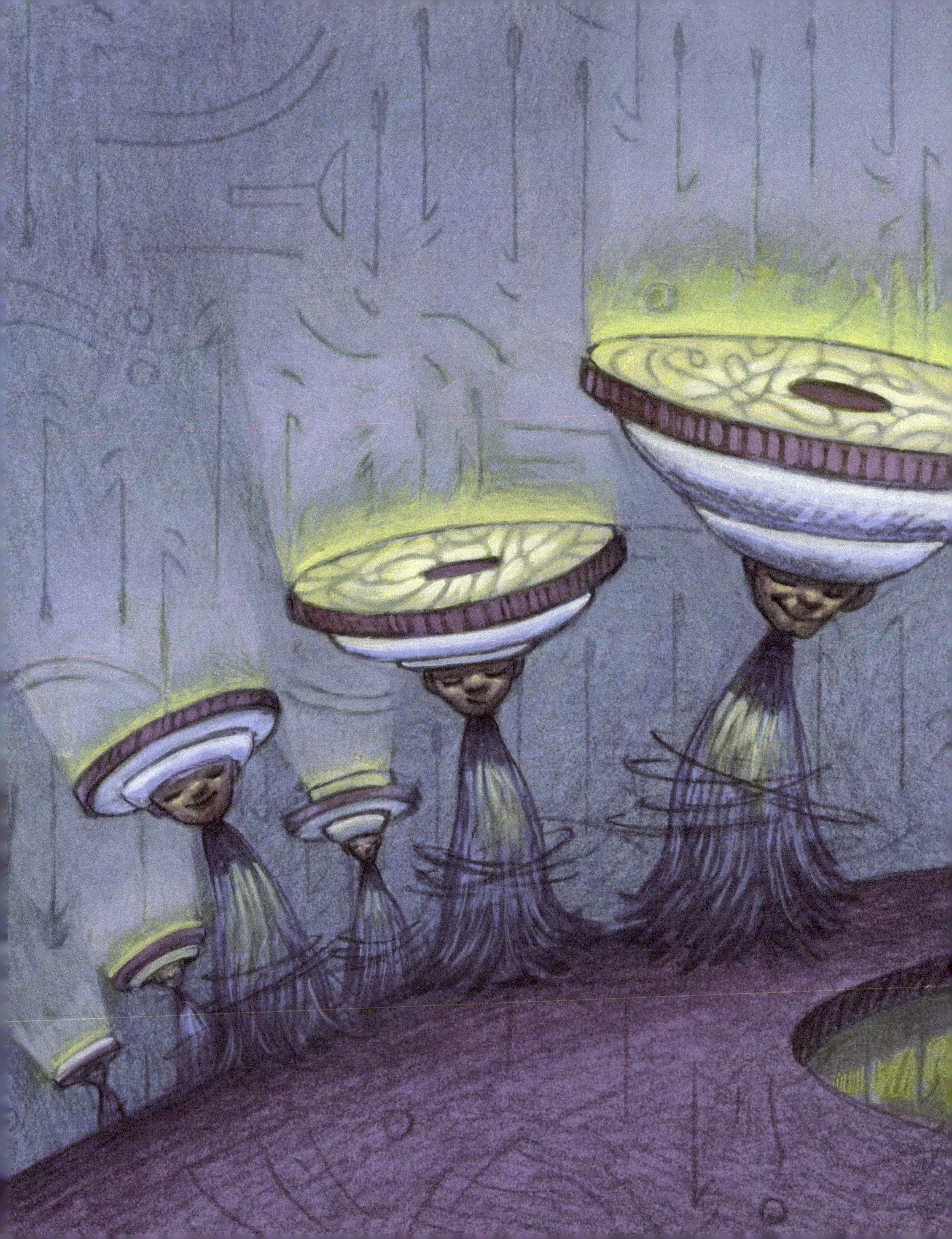

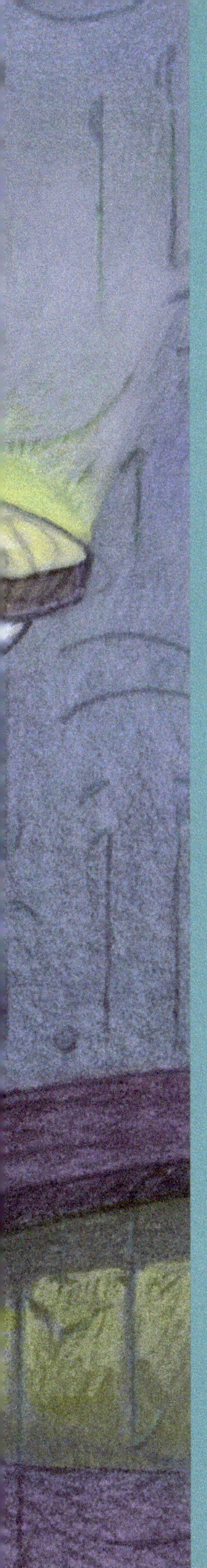

CHAPTER 16

HELP THEM SEE

I often hesitate when someone asks, *"What do you do?"* I guess technically speaking, my position is administrator, but this doesn't seem completely right. In response, I tend to stutter as I cycle through the other things I do and wonder which one to share – well, I am an artist, teacher, writer, leader, etc. I am sure my hesitation makes them wonder if I somehow forgot, or if I am just making stuff up!

What do you do? Are you considered faculty? (a teacher, professor, instructor, etc.) Or maybe you are in a leadership position? (a chair, dean, director, etc.) Perhaps it doesn't really matter. *If you are a teacher – be a leader too. If you are a leader, teach.* Regardless of position or title, in creative leadership the two disciplines of teaching and leadership are inextricably connected.

These two disciplines are brought together by a significant leadership belief described in Chapter 4. Here it is again: Belief #3: Followers have potential to become leaders. With this as our core belief, a big part of our job as a creative leader is to teach and mentor others to become creative leaders. We can teach them to see, think, and act in a way that will help them achieve their fullest potential.

What does "teaching" look like for a creative leader? Teaching or instructing means you may be actively offering information, sharing experience, or explaining a topic – using the modes of visual thinking to engage the imagination. You might be providing instructions or expounding on principles of a design, while teaching the design thinking process. You might be posing the BIG questions. In the end, what you teach is intended to develop their creative vision.

This chapter will describe the teaching philosophy of a creative leader. It is founded on the three aspects of creative vision we discussed in Chapters 5 and 6. Leaders who teach help group members expand their creative vision to see the future (and themselves) with an eye of faith. They prompt them to identify the gaps in their learning, and understand the systems, structures, relationships, and components at play. This philosophy can be applied to a wide range of teaching scenarios and is not specific to the university classroom or professional training opportunities.

THE TEACHING OF A CREATIVE LEADER

Creative leaders teach in formal and informal ways. For the purposes of this discussion, the teaching philosophy below is most relevant in the context of a "course" – any formal teaching opportunity that has a defined scope, purpose, and curriculum.

If you approach your teaching opportunities as a creative leader, your teaching philosophy might read like this:

> My primary objective as a teacher is to help my students to clarify, trust, and accomplish their vision. To do this, I help them see themselves with great creative potential, understand the context of what they are learning, and define their own vision. I offer broad-based resources and vision-based feedback. I ask the right questions and illuminate the subject with visuals and metaphors. I give them space to work, to ask questions, and to experiment as they apply what they are learning.

Help Them See:

In the early stages of the learning experience, students will have two primary concerns: They want to know: 1) What is the point of this course? 2) Do I have what it takes to succeed? More than just going over the course description or syllabus, help them see the context of the course, how it fits into the big picture, and how it relates to the discipline, domain, or organization. If there are expectations, components, systems, or processes that they need to understand, explain them early and often.

It is important for them to be reminded of their unique potential to be successful, in this course and beyond. Get to know them and learn what approach will best engage their imagination. Share your vision and help them see themselves with great creative potential.

Clarify Their Vision:
Within the objectives of the course, give your students the freedom to set their own creative vision and work toward it. Engage them in activities that will clarify their creative vision. Design activities to focus the student on what they truly want and remove barriers or preconceived notions about how to achieve it. Encourage them to focus on the results *they* want (not what you want), and to ignore concerns about the "how" (the means that may be used to accomplish the results). That will come later. Together, address their fears and validate their creative vision.

Offer Resources:
Once the results have been chosen, the resources needed to accomplish the vision become more apparent. With a clear vision in mind, the student will begin to see the relevant information, skills, tools, and other resources they will need to accomplish it. This is the best time to teach and offer resources.

Students need broad-based resources to help them understand the field or domain that they are working in. Offer a wide knowledge base of the people, theories, studies, and happenings that are informing our current understanding and conditions. Tell stories, give presentations, require reading, and expect a high level of research.

In addition, provide information, demonstrate techniques, introduce tools, and teach skills that are vision-based. This means that what you offer is directly related to what the student needs to accomplish their vision. The students are now feeling creative tension, and any tools we can provide to help them leverage it are highly relevant. In addition to instruction, work to provide timely and pertinent feedback whenever possible. Tailor the feedback schedule and use critiques, responses, and grades to provide feedback to the student at critical stages of their learning.

Ask the Right Questions:
The critical skill of a teacher is knowing the right questions to ask and when to ask them. You might ask a question to assess the student's knowledge, prompt a discussion, or to encourage analysis. Avoid fact-based questions as those tend to put a student on the spot and focus their mind on retaining facts, figures, or dates. If the question seems too obvious, they might wonder if it is a trick question. Instead, carefully *design* each question. To do this well, consider the purpose of each question you want to ask. It takes time and intention but will yield deeper discussions and learning.

In your course, you should not be the only one asking questions. Strive to create a culture that gives space for every question. Students should feel empowered to ask BIG questions and to question the status quo. Design compelling questions to engage their imagination, and challenge questions to activate the creative potential that is inherent (but sometimes dormant) in each student.

Illuminate the Subject:
As the pressure of preparing to teach begins to build, you might not feel that there is time to get creative or imaginative with your teaching. Just remember that whatever efforts you make to illuminate the subject for your students will be well worth the return on student engagement.

Instead of falling into the trap of text-heavy, linear presentations, look for engaging ways to use pictures, drawings, videos, prototypes, stories, and metaphors to deliver information.

Give them Space to Innovate:
There are certain factors that contribute to learning which seem to be in direct contrast with the structures of the academic classroom or other learning opportunities. Learning often requires failure, practice, and experimentation. Ironically, grading and evaluating performance often discourages this type of exploration. Find a way to reward people for growth, not for outcomes. As a result, you will show them that you value learning and innovation, over proficiency.

Finding the right methods and learning the appropriate skills to accomplish their vision is often a matter of experimentation. However, students gravitate to their comfort zones, being afraid to make mistakes and receive a poor grade. To counter this, create a culture of innovation where experimentation is rewarded, even celebrated. This gives them freedom to take risks and explore.

THE GIFTS OF TEACHING

If you are like me, you seek out honest feedback from those you teach. You want to make sure that your teaching is hitting the mark. But what is the mark? When you get feedback, what do you look for? Is it just to see if they like you as a leader or teacher?

The mark of good teaching for a creative leader is evidence of the gifts of teaching. If you can see the influence of these gifts, it means you have truly empowered that person to grow and get closer to their vision.

So, the next time you get some feedback on your teaching, read between the lines and look for clarity, choice, relevance, motivation, and freedom. Embedded in your student's comments will be subtle indications that they have received your gifts.

Gift of Clarity: As you describe the big picture and then expect a student to develop a clear vision, you are giving them the gift of clarity. They will come to understand why they are in the course and what they really want.

Gift of Choice: When you extend and share a wide knowledge base of the people, theories, studies, and happenings in the discipline with your students you might think that you are offering them knowledge. In reality, you are giving them the gift of choice and empowering them to choose the information that they will need to reach their potential.

Gift of Relevance: As you help a student see the gap (or discrepancy) between their vision and their current reality, you are making the information they need highly relevant to their needs.

Gift of Motivation: When you effectively design, frame, or inspire questions so that your students will seek to discover the answer, you are giving them the gift of motivation.

Gift of Freedom: Giving your students space to question and to choose, and allowing for practice, failure, and experimentation, will actually give your students the freedom to learn from their mistakes.

Whether you are a teacher who leads groups to their vision, or a leader who teaches new ways of thinking, I invite you to step back and analyze your teaching. Are you bringing your imagination into the work? Are you honoring the creativity and imagination of those you teach? Are you designing for success and incorporating visual thinking strategies into the lesson plan? Lastly, have you offered them the gifts of teaching?

CHAPTER 17

ILLUMINATE WITH METAPHORS

Throughout this book, we have been discussing the ways that a creative leader can make abstract ideas visible and develop creative vision in others. One significant way to do this is through metaphor. Again, this is about relationships. Creative leaders can develop the unique ability to help us see the relationships between two concepts that don't appear to have any connection at first.

Daniel Pink wrote the following in his book called *A Whole New Mind:*

> "Metaphor – that is, understanding one thing in terms of something else – is another important element of Symphony. In a complex world, mastery of metaphor – a whole-minded ability that some cognitive scientists have called 'imaginative rationality' – has become ever more valuable."[61]

"Symphony" is one of Daniel Pink's conceptual age senses. He argues that after generations in the linear thinking of the information age – we need a whole new set of aptitudes for the conceptual age. We have talked about the idea of Symphony already, though we did not call it that. We called it systems thinking.

In an actual symphony, the conductor and musicians try to bring different sounds and instruments together into harmonious or purposeful relationships. However, as Daniel Pink explains:

> "...perfecting those relationships – important though it is – is not the ultimate goal of their efforts... What separates the long remembered from the quickly forgotten is the ability to marshal these relationships into a whole whose magnificence exceeds the sum of its parts. So it is with the high-concept aptitude of Symphony. The boundary crosser, the inventor, and the metaphor maker all understand the importance of relationships. But the Conceptual Age also demands the ability to grasp the relationships between relationships. This meta-ability goes by many names – systems thinking, gestalt thinking, holistic thinking. I prefer to think of it simply as seeing the big picture."[62]

[61] Daniel Pink, A Whole New Mind (New York: Riverhead Books/Penguin, 2005), 140.

Of course, the *big picture* is yet another metaphor. A creative leader will utilize metaphor to help others see the big picture, or the system, or the structures. Here I describe two metaphors that may be helpful to your work and your teaching.

THE SCRABBLE PRINCIPLE

The Scrabble Principle is a metaphor for how individuals can relate to and collaborate with others who are also playing the game. It may help us to look beyond ourselves and see connections or opportunities around us.

When my kids were younger, I set out to teach them how to play Scrabble. When we first started, they would focus intently on the seven tiles they had randomly selected at the beginning of their turn. Usually, they were able to make a small three- or four-letter word and then would excitedly wait for their turn to play it. Very often however, they would start their turn and then realize that they had nowhere on the Scrabble board to place their word. As you may know, you can't just choose the best scoring possibility and place a complete word on the board. Instead, you must build on words that are already in place.

Watching my children's tendency to focus too much on their own set of tiles and then struggle to find a way to connect with the ever-changing Scrabble board, led me to an interesting realization. I was doing exactly the same thing in my own work. As an illustrator, I believed that if I could just make a great illustration (or maybe even the best illustration!), I would score a lot of "points" and be very successful. As the director of a non-profit, I believed that if I could just make a great fund-

[62] Daniel Pink, A Whole New Mind, 141.

raiser or program – with our small but dedicated team – that we would eventually bring in enough people and raise enough money.

I was typically disappointed. The artwork seemed to be limited in exposure and somewhat predictable, certainly not unique in the marketplace. The fundraisers were often attended only by the committee and the staff – oh, and a few of their friends. Despite my best efforts to innovate my process or promote our program, the results all looked the same and produced the same outcomes.

The Scrabble Principle changed all of that for me. The Scrabble Principle is based on the idea of connecting the unconnected. I decided that in order to be more successful in art, business, and life, I would have to start making connections to good "words" that are already placed on the Scrabble board. I started to see the Scrabble board as a metaphor for the "public domain" or the "marketplace." The place where ideas existed.

Each part of the game plays an important role in this extended metaphor:

Words on the board: In my mind, the words on the Scrabble board represent the creations, contributions, or products (even ideas) that live in the public domain.

Tiles: Just like Scrabble tiles, each of us has a random set of resources or assets we can use to accomplish our work. These tiles may come in the form of natural talent, developed skills, and/or people that come into our lives.

Other Players: If you stop and think about what is happening in the game, you realize that you cannot build your word without building on what someone else has done. The other players are not our competition. *They are our partners.*

Rules of the Game: The rules provide the structure we need to operate within. Rules are simply limiting factors that represent the reality of life and leadership. We are all limited in some way by policy, time constraints, or the status quo.

Points: Within the structure of every game is some form of feedback that lets you know how you are doing. In a game like Scrabble, this is usually in the form of points. "Points" or feedback in life can come in a variety of forms, including money, compliments, social media followers, etc. We can look for ways to measure the effectiveness of the "words" we build.

Of course, in the game of Scrabble there is often a clear winner, and the rest of us feel like losers. But when collaboration happens in life and work, everybody can win. You bring your seven tiles to the table, and I bring mine. We build on the contributions of each other, recognizing them as fundamental to our success.

The power of this metaphor is apparent when we use it to make connections that we did not see before. On the next page is a series of questions that you can ask yourself whenever you have a need for creating a new "word" (i.e., initiative, program, course, etc.).

In my case, by thinking in this way, I was able to completely change my artistic style and become more competitive in the marketplace.

Collaborating with a good friend and others in the community, I was able to illustrate, design, self-publish, promote, and sell a picture book that did very well in our local market. The images from the book strengthened my portfolio which led to additional work as an illustrator and the opportunity to work with a new artist representative.

In a world of distinct disciplines and separate silos, the creative leader must win by seeing the whole "game board," turning other players into partners, and creating new solutions to old problems by connecting the unconnected.

THE LABYRINTH AND THE PATH

Some time ago, when I was the Chair of Art and Design at the Community College of Aurora, I taught a class called Creativity and Visual Thinking. The course was designed to introduce students to the components of the creative process and encourage them to be an active creative participant, instead of a passive learner.

Imagine a course where students told stories, engaged in design challenges, made music together with random household objects, explored unseen forces at play by playing the stick game, built newspaper bridges that were strong enough to hold a stack of books, and created guardian figures out of any media they wanted. It was fun!

As the textbook for the course, I chose a book by Daniel Pink called A Whole New Mind (mentioned earlier). We studied and discussed the six senses that help us move beyond the outdated linear thinking of the past. When we explored the chapter on meaning, I wanted to help students reflect on their learning and create meaning; so one of the projects we did (as a class) was to create a labyrinth.

And you might know, a labyrinth is not a maze. You get lost in a maze and you can't get out. It's a very frustrating and very analytical process. A labyrinth, on the other hand, guides you through to the center, and then walks you back out. You don't have to think about where you are going, you just walk, and it guides you through.

The labyrinth is designed to provide a path of least resistance, that leads you right to the center. Walking a labyrinth is sort of like doing the dishes, mowing the lawn, or taking a shower. Your analytical brain is activated but free from making decisions and other parts of your brain can open up to the challenges that you are facing. When you follow the path of least resistance you find yourself a little more centered, and clear about what you want. So, we created a labyrinth at the end of each course to reflect on our learning, and discuss ways to find meaning in our work.

You might not create a labyrinth for your team, but you can encourage them to reflect on their process, find clarity about their purpose, or to create meaning in their own work. In addition, you might think about the labyrinth as a metaphor for how you design your classroom, workplace, and projects.

What is the path of least resistance for your project or course? Does the structure or the borders of the work – including projects, visuals, and discussions – naturally lead your team or students to where you want them to go?

As you step back and open yourself up to possibilities, you will learn to create your own metaphors. They will help you engage with your students in new and interesting ways.

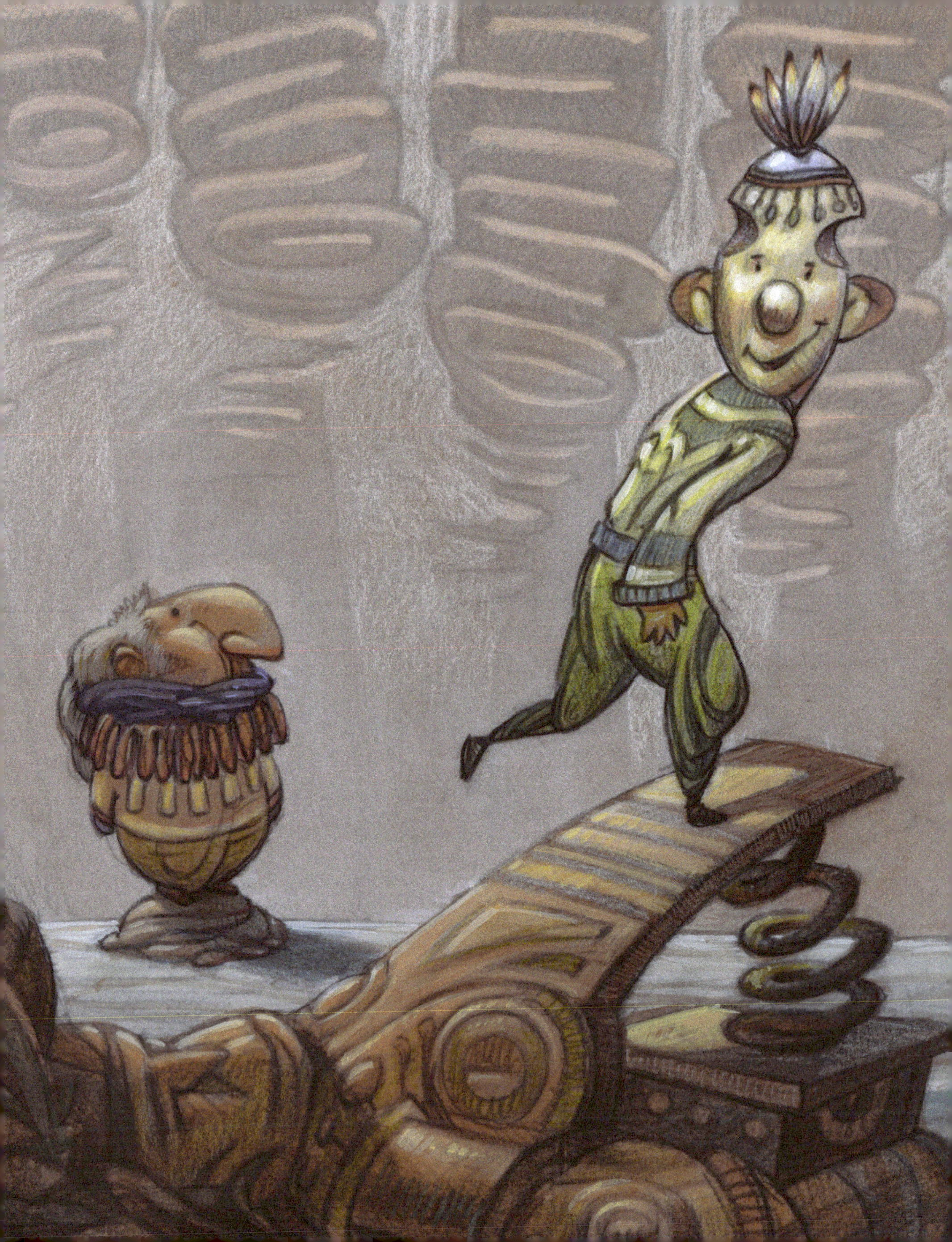

CHAPTER 18

QUESTION THE STATUS QUO

On my first day as the Chair of Illustration at Rocky Mountain College of Art + Design, two things caught my eye in the faculty office. The first was a gift from the faculty – a welcome note and a bottle of linseed oil. During the interview process they learned that instead of using proper linseed oil to thin my oil paints, I used regular cooking oil. I guess I am not a purist when it comes to traditional painting techniques. Cooking oil is cheaper, and I don't like the fumes from the fancy stuff. Vegetable oil works just fine for my purposes. The only downside? All my paintings smell like french fries.

The second thing that I noticed was a quote written on the wall. It read, *"Tradition is the springboard for innovation."* This phrase was put there by the previous chair. You know that it must have been very important to be written on the wall, but the longer I thought about it, the quote began to raise several questions for me. I wondered if it was meant to justify the program's position of continuing to teach traditional ways of working – in the face of emerging technologies.

Don't get me wrong, we need tradition. Especially in making art that is intended to be understood. In illustration, we have established certain principles and methods that are effective in leading the eye and telling the story. We teach these principles and expect to see them in student work.

But we don't expect every student to use traditional tools or to choose realism as their method of working. In fact, we expect them to *innovate*.

The question then becomes, *"What causes a student to jump on the springboard of tradition?"* After we have driven home traditional ideals and practices, what would cause them to let go of all that and jump for innovation? And what exactly is our job as educators? Is it to simply teach the tradition? Have we done our job if we can say, "Here is your tradition springboard – we have taught you what it looks like, how tall it is, and how it was constructed. Enjoy!"

No. Handing students a metaphorical springboard on the day of graduation is not enough. We need to teach them how to jump.

A creative leader will expect those they teach to jump. Actually – they will *challenge* them to jump and then give them space to innovate. They will coach them through their practice runs, measure their growth, and help them define their vision. They will train them to let go of fear, comparison, and ideas about their past so that they can build creative momentum.

Whether we are talking about students or group members on our team, leading them toward innovation is one of the three expansive actions that a creative leader employs at the synthesis level. It is an approach to leadership and teaching that embraces the imagination at every moment. As a person with influence, you arrange the systems and structures so that the path of least resistance for your group guides them to creative success.

So far, we have discussed two of the three expansive actions that Creative Leaders take to maximize creative results. As a reminder, here are the three actions: 1) Develop Vision, 2) Close the Gap, and 3) Lead for Innovation. This next section will discuss some of the ways that you can lead for innovation – starting with how you can ask the right questions.

ASK THE RIGHT QUESTIONS

As creative leaders, we facilitate great ideas through great questions. Whether you are working with a team of faculty or a group of students, if you want them to innovate – carefully designing a question, prompt, or line of inquiry is a great way to engage their imagination. Or better yet, you could help them come up with their own questions that will inspire investigation and innovation.

So, what are the right questions?

Ask BIG questions

In this case, BIG means deep, fundamental, broad, or even unanswerable. Every discipline or endeavor seems to have these types of compelling questions that need to be asked. Often they have a way of touching our deep, fundamental, core beliefs about ourselves and the universe.

It seems that the bigger the question, the more we feel compelled to answer it. Usually, if you are asking a BIG question of your team, it is not because you have the answer. It is because you share the desire with your team to try to answer it. Or, because you want to use that question to explain the framework, context, or system that your team is working in.

Questions to Understand

The primary purpose of any question is to gain understanding. If you have ulterior motives for asking a question, the person you are asking may become wary, even defensive. When a creative leader questions *"Why?,"* we are just trying to learn about our current reality. We are trying to see and understand the systems and structures. We want to know why something is the way that it is.

Too many of us don't bother asking for an explanation. We simply accept our current reality and don't really understand it. If we want to move past our current reality, we

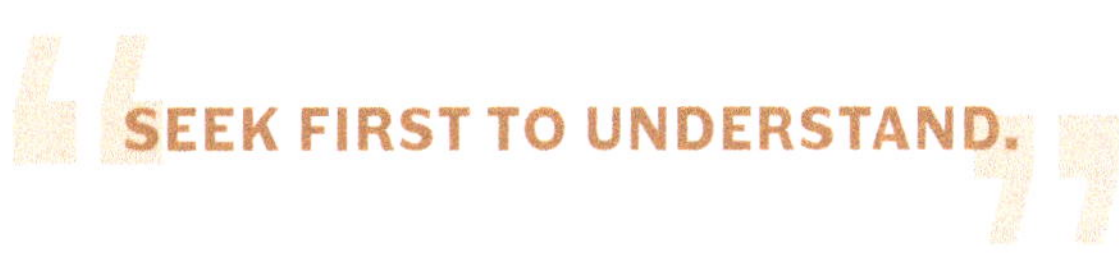

have to know it – and be honest about where we are. As we seek to improve our current reality, we don't   need to be contrarians who question everything or are always dissatisfied and grumpy. Instead, we just need to ask enough questions to understand our starting point and how it relates to the vision we seek to create.

Vision-based Questions

After we have a solid understanding of current reality, our questions should be about vision. What is our vision? Do we have a clear idea of what we want? Do we know where we are headed? If you are in a subordinate role, ask questions until you truly understand where the leader wants to go. This will help them define and clarify their vision. You can also ask questions to help form the vision. Usually these are questions about the end user. Who are we really designing for? What do they want? How can we prototype this idea, etc.?

Another type of vision-based question is any question that shows others that you understand the vision and that your question is intended to move the group closer to the desired outcome. How can I help us get there? Help me better understand…? These types of questions will lead you toward the vision and will prompt further questions from the group.

Status Quo Questions

When I was at a community college in the Denver area, we had two campuses. One was a retired military base with long rectangular buildings and retrofitted classrooms. Early in my tenure, I walked past a large break room that used to be a machine shop. It had large windows into the hallway, a wide assortment of mis-matched furniture, and a large free-standing television from the 1990s. It seemed like the place where outdated furniture went to die before it was finally thrown out. I was told that students used it as a break room.

Over a couple of months, I would periodically check to see if the space was being used. More often than not, it was completely empty. Or maybe one or two students were eating lunch and watching daytime television. As you walked upstairs from this breakroom, you would see a desk in the small hallway foyer at the top of the stairs. This was where our administrative assistant sat, it was just outside of my office and in a place that was visible to students.

The last thing that you need to know is that even though we were a visual arts program, we did not have a designated gallery space. We did not have a place to gather or host visiting artists. Can you see where I am going with this?

And so, I started asking questions to understand current reality. *"Why is the administrative assistant sitting in the hall? What are we using the break room for? Where did all this furniture come from? Does the college have any future plans for this space?"*

Once I felt like I fully understood the decisions we made that got us to that point, I started asking questions that started with *"What if..."* What if we created a gallery space in the old breakroom? What if we moved the administrative assistant into that space to tend the gallery and have a way to lock up their office? What if we built modular walls to increase the usable wall space? What if we brought in guest artists to exhibit their work and interact with our students? Is there a donor in the community that would like to see this space as a gallery? In time, we answered each question and part-nered with a member of the board to develop a beautiful gallery space for our students.

> **SOME MEN SEE THINGS AS THEY ARE, AND ASK WHY. I DREAM OF THINGS THAT NEVER WERE, AND ASK WHY NOT.**
>
> – Bobby Kennedy

All the "what if" questions had led us to a new reality. A much better status quo! If I had never asked those questions things would have stayed the same, moderately useful but certainly not meaningful. The space would never have become a transformative learning space where our community interacted with art and with each other.

Challenge Questions

A huge part of creative leadership is fostering innovation from those you lead. As leaders we might be tempted to tell our team what to do. But that is no way to strengthen their imagination or improve their creative skills. A better way is to provide a challenge or prompt that lays out the issue that needs to be solved, describes the parameters that group members are working under, and invites them to apply their imagination to the project.

Creative leaders use various forms of challenge questions to activate the creative potential that is inherent (but sometimes dormant) in our teams. A challenge question is carefully designed to frame the design problem and guide the team through their work. If the question is designed well it can lead the group to innovative solutions.

What makes a good challenge question? The team at IDEO suggests that a good challenge question starts with "How might we..." This format works well because even in three short words it suggests some powerful concepts. "How" encourages a discussion about process, but also focuses the group on the stated vision that completes the sentence. "Might" is optimistic and open to possibilities. "We" calls for collaboration from all involved.

Here are a few more tips from IDEO for crafting a strong challenge question.

[63] From my notes from a course called "Designing for Change" at IDEO U.

Constant Questions (don't stop asking questions!)

Stay curious. As a creative leader, you can use questions to establish context, understand current reality, question the status quo, and challenge your team to engage their imaginations. But questions to inspire innovation do not stop when the challenge has been laid out. Hundreds of additional questions should be posed throughout the project (from everyone on the team) to clarify, encourage, and engage. What if? What else? Have you thought about this? Why did that work? What idea resonates with you? What story do you want your end user to tell?

SUMMARY:

As we wrap up this section on questions, here is a word of caution. Poorly designed or poorly timed questions can be disruptive to the creative process. It is important to sense where the team is at in their process. Start by asking questions that provide you with context into the status of the project. Once you have a clear idea of the progress that has been made, you can avoid questions that are no longer relevant. It is likely that some things have already been decided and the team has moved on.

If you want to contribute to the process moving forward, take some time to discover the issues that the team is still wrestling with. Design your questions to acknowledge the progress and inspire the next steps. Be careful to communicate trust in your team and explain the purpose of your questions. You are not questioning the person, their intent, or their personality; so make sure that your questions do not come across as a personal attack.

CHAPTER 19

MAKE SPACE FOR INNOVATION

More than anything else, leading for innovation means that you design, create, and maintain an environment or culture where innovation is the norm, the expectation, even the path of least resistance. This takes time and intention to develop – and will lead to unforeseen developments and meaningful learning experiences. As a leader in a team or organization, you can create a culture that engages the imagination and leads people toward their creative vision.

Creating culture is a *bit* different from creating art. You can't manipulate people the same way that you shape clay or push paint. Peter Senge acknowledged this as well. He wrote,

> "When we think of ourselves as designers, it might even be tempting to think of the organization as a sort of machine, one that somehow needs to be redesigned. But, we are participants in the system not outsiders, and you do not redesign a living system as you would redesign an automobile. Leaders who appreciate organizations as living systems approach design work differently."[64]

So, what is culture? Right now, it's a buzzword in organizational leadership. But I see it as a collection of norms, i.e., attitudes and behaviors that constitute the *unwritten* rules of a team or organization.

CULTURE IS CREATED BY:

- What we expect
- What we make space for
- What we celebrate

As a leader, what do you expect?

During one class, I told the students we would be going on a field trip. They were excited! Then I walked them over to a large vacant lot between buildings. It was not what they were expecting. But I expected them to dream big! When we arrived, I said: *"You walk past this section*

[64] Peter Senge, The Fifth Discipline, 321.

of the campus nearly every day. Did you ever stop to think about what this could be?" They hadn't.

Their assignment was to envision something new for that space and write up their unique vision. Our discussion generated a range of very practical to highly-imaginative ideas for what we could do with that space. They suggested a sculpture garden, an amphitheater, a moving sidewalk to get to class, and new restaurants for the campus community. Some of the ideas had great potential with the right resources.

Creative leaders establish culture by defining their expectations. Whether it is with students or your team, you can expect them to dream big. You can invite others to think for themselves and generate unique creative ideas.

What do you make space for?
During our discussion about design thinking in Chapter 10, we learned that project teams need space to innovate. There are a couple of ways to think about "space." The first is actual, physical space. Is there a space that you can dedicate to those parts of the design process that call for ideation, visioning, or for dreaming big? Setting aside a physical space is a visual and physical reminder of what you value. It can be an intentional way of creating the culture you want to see in your classroom or organization.

A second way to think about space is as emotional or psychological space. Is there safe space in your conversations and meetings for new ideas? Are you asking your team to engage their imagination and to innovate? Or are new ideas discouraged by territorialism, oppressive policies, workload concerns, or jealousy? Is there room for team members to take risks and make mistakes?

When I was at the community college, I felt free to experiment and take risks with my creativity class. I mentioned how at the end of the course, we would create a labyrinth. But I didn't mention my attempt at a world record! One day I decided that I wanted to create a living labyrinth. A labyrinth where the path was defined by people (mostly students, but some faculty and administrators) laying on the ground end to end, head to toe. I calculated that I would need 70 people and I put out flyers to promote the event. It was a great success and we had a lot of fun.

So, obviously the next step was to do it bigger and better, and create the world's largest living labyrinth. I applied with the Guinness organization, though I wasn't exactly sure how to categorize a human labyrinth. Apparently, they weren't sure either. When I pestered them for a response, they simply said: *"We don't have a category for that."*

What!? Have you seen their book? They have categories for everything! Like many organizations, they need to make more space for innovation.

It is interesting how ideas, concepts, and even physical objects can take up emotional or conceptual space. Making space might also mean letting go of something or throwing it out. When we get rid of a tired idea or tradition, we make space for something else.

There are many good strategies to lead your group to imaginative ideas and innovation. One that we often forget is: Play. Creative leaders play and learn to make space for play. As you strive to create a culture of learning and innovation, you might have to teach others how to engage in creative play – to make, or do, or think just for fun. This might seem a little counter intuitive when our work time is so precious, but play will bring positive emotions, spark new ideas, and encourage experimentation.

Most children are experts in play. Mr. Fred Rogers said, "...for children, play is serious learning." [65] It can be the same for adult learners as well. If you can get them playing, they will also be learning. And so, why not? Why not make it fun? As Jamie Runnells explained, "If creative play brings joy, fosters innovation, is serious learning/serious work, and fosters courage, it stands to reason that it should be a regular part of every creative practice."[66]

[65] Fred Rogers, Why Play is the Work of Childhood (Latrobe PA: The Fred Rogers Center, available at: https://www.fredrogerscenter.org/2014/09/why-play-is-the-work-of-childhood/, 2018).

[66] Jamie Runnells, "A Case for Creative Play" (ICON 11 Illustration Conference, June 30, 2022).

But creative, intentional play might not organically show up in the classroom or the committee meeting. You will have to design for it. You might even have to schedule it. When my wife and I were first dating we noticed a difference in our personalities. She was fun and spontaneous. I was thoughtful and scheduled. One day, she teasingly suggested, *You should be more spontaneous! Just do whatever!* I smiled and said, *That's a great idea, maybe I can schedule some time for that!* After that, we called it "scheduled spontaneity." It was the time when I would decide to be spontaneous. In a similar way, creative leaders can make space for play.

Is there space on your calendar for play or experimentation? If you want to create a culture of innovation, a good way to begin is to get it on the calendar. If it never makes it to the calendar, it will likely never get done. You can tell a lot about your priorities by evaluating the meetings on your calendar. If most of your time is spent managing and maintaining the day-to-day, it will be hard to find time to step back and think long-term, or to playfully experiment with a vision of a better future in mind.

What do you celebrate?

Celebrating is an intentional way to nudge the culture of your organization. Many of us are good at celebrating milestones (like anniversaries or birthdays) or the completion of a project.

But creative leaders learn to celebrate imagination, patience, and collaboration – our super-components, as a way to guide the culture toward innovation. Usually, these components are not seen or remembered at the end of the project or process – so find a way to celebrate in the moment, whenever you see them show up. You can do this by providing positive feedback, reaffirming core values of the creative process, and letting the group know that they are meeting expectations.

Results are important to recognize and celebrate, but creative leaders also celebrate learning – even if it comes by way of failure. Learning can be harder to identify and recognize, but a culture of innovation is powered by celebrating constant curiosity.

– Jamie Runnells

When I was teaching my first illustration course as a graduate student at Utah State University, I wanted us to celebrate collaboration. It seems that single-image illustration, by its nature, is pretty much a solo activity. As a children's book illustrator, I would rarely work with the writer of the text that I was illustrating. Sometimes I would share an idea with the art director, but most times the work is not very collaborative.

I thought it would be great to get my students to work together on a collaborative project. And so for this project, we sat around a table and started brainstorming together. As a group, we chose a song by *The Decemberists* that the students wanted to bring to life. Throughout the process, we employed everyone's strengths. One student did the initial sketches, others did final line drawings and then paintings. Another student made some puppets, someone designed backgrounds, and a student with technical media skills brought it all together as a music video for the song.

As the instructor, I had created the space for innovation, expected collaboration, and then let students inform the process. I carefully designed the grading structure to reward learning and collaboration. I guided them through the project, asking questions, and pointing out learning opportunities.

With some intentionality, you can do this too! If you are an instructor, design some space within your course for collaboration. Allow your students to inform the project and the process. If you take an active role in the project, they will see themselves as partners in a creative process. At first, they might be unsure about this. Power dynamics can make it challenging for teachers and students to see each other as partners. But you can choose to collaborate and embrace this meaningful experience. When you do, you will be offering your students the gifts of freedom and motivation.

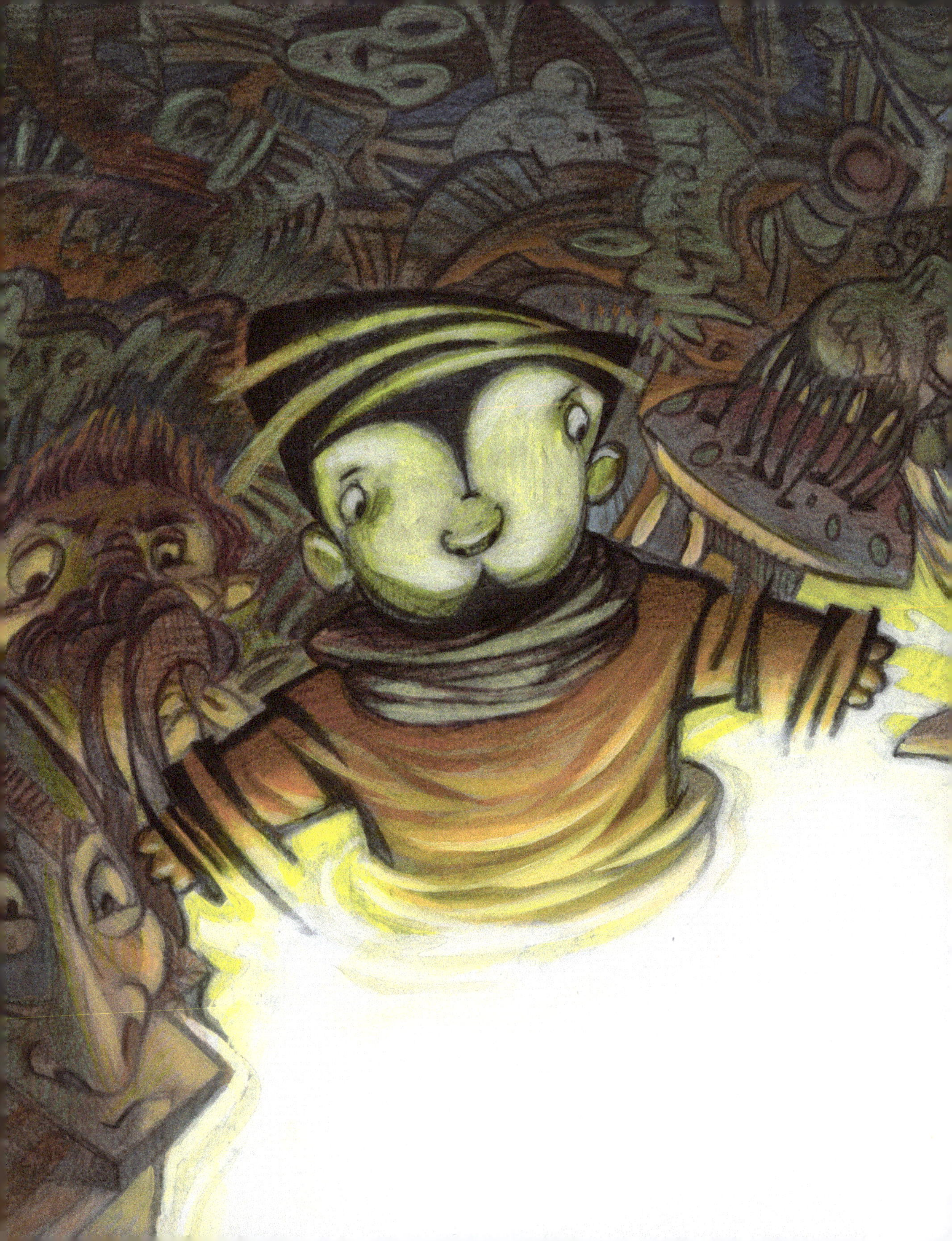

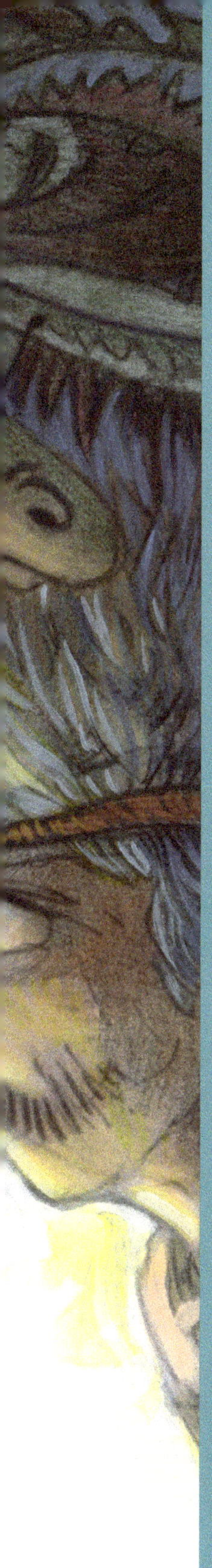

CHAPTER 20

CREATIVE SYNTHESIS

Earlier in the book, we described the creative leadership framework as a powerful engine composed of many parts working together to drive us toward our vision. As the concepts of the book have unfolded, we have removed each one from the framework and examined them carefully.

As we conclude, let's study this third level of the framework a bit more. We will see that it includes the three expansive actions: developing vision, closing the gap, and leading for innovation.

At the fundamental level and strategic level our creative work is mostly internal in nature. It has to do with belief, imagination, and planning – all happening in our minds. This type of activity is called "thinking toward creation."

The third level is heavy with action and obvious manifestations (or results) of our imagination. Taking creative action at this level is called "working toward creation." It is no longer about developing our core beliefs or imagination – its relying on them. It's not about strategizing or planning – it's about making our thinking visible. Anytime you take discernable creative action (a step designed to bring you closer to your vision), you are operating in the synthesis level.

Since the structure of this book is linear and we can only discuss one idea at a time, it might seem like each of these actions and strategies is meant to be applied separately or in a certain order. They are not. Instead, there is an opportunity here for simultaneous integration of each level into our work – an experience called synthesis. Creativity at the synthesis level is described as the fusion of creative beliefs, thinking strategies, and expansive actions. Creative leaders harmonize and integrate each component as they lead others toward accomplishing their vision.

Synthesis sounds fancy, but it is simply another way to say that we are practicing creative leadership. When we synthesize, we put these concepts into action and apply each manifestation of our imagination toward the completion of our vision. We make stuff to prototype our ideas, bring personal expression into our teaching, and find ways to leverage creative tension. This is not flashy, surface-level creativity – it is synthesis-level creativity, the kind that brings our vision into being. This is true innovation.

VISUALIZING CREATIVE LEADERSHIP

As you consider the framework, you will notice that the three levels seem be stacked upon each other. This is representative of the ways that imaginative fundamentals, thinking strategies, and expansive actions integrate with each other – becoming one comprehensive strategy for leadership. There may be more we can learn about creative leadership as we visualize the dynamic nature of the framework. For example, what happens if we enlarge, compress, or rotate the framework?

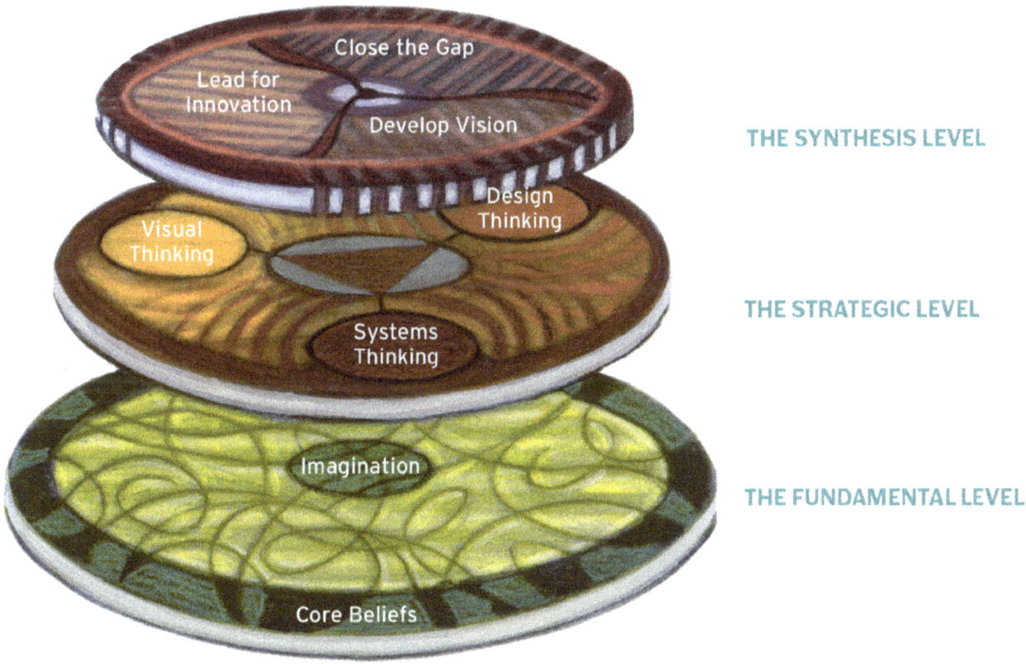

Imagine our framework as a three-dimensional model floating in front of you. It is slowly rotating in space with light glancing off the colors on the top level. You can see the labels that call out the thinking strategies and the expansive actions. In your mind's eye, reach out and grab the fundamental level with both hands. Gently pull it from both sides to enlarge it.

This is essentially what you were doing in the first section as you examined your core beliefs and chose mindsets that enlarged your creative potential. As you do this, the other two levels expand at the same time. Since the imagination is fundamental to all creative activity, its expansion will affect the entire framework. You will now have more imaginative capacity to apply to your leadership.

Now imagine what happens when you compress the levels together. Push the synthesis level down, bring the fundamental level up. Now you can feel the framework in your hands as a large, round disk. This brings everything closer together. The levels are still identifiable, but they influence each other more immediately.

The imagination is now more connected to the expansive actions you take as you work toward your vision. You might note that "visual thinking" lines up directly under and is now touching "lead for innovation." And rightfully so, since visual thinking is a very effective strategy for leading others toward innovation. Using the modes of visual thinking, we can help others see, understand, and share our vision of the future.

"Systems Thinking" now has a stronger connection with "Develop Vision" and that is seen in the framework as we compress the levels and bring them together. This is consistent with the idea that we can enhance our creative vision by using the diagrams and symbols of systems thinking. We can develop creative vision in others by helping them see systems, structures, relationships, and forces at play. In a similar way, design thinking now touches "close the gap" and we can consider ways those two concepts interact and influence each other.

While the levels are now compressed, they are still distinct, and we can explore additional movement within the framework. Imagine that you are now holding the framework disk in the upright palm of your hand. Use your other hand to rotate the synthesis level – like taking the lid off of a jar. What connections are made if we rotate this level upon the center axis? If you rotate clockwise, "close the gap" will move over "visual thinking." And suddenly a whole new set of relationships, concepts, and questions become apparent, with the most prominent question being – *"How can I use visual thinking to help close the gap?"*

With this in mind, you are invited to rotate the synthesis level and look for new connections. Questions like these will open our minds to a range of new ideas and connections.

A FEW QUESTIONS TO GET YOU STARTED:

- How might we apply design thinking as a mechanism for meaningful innovation?

- How might we use visual thinking to lead for innovation and overcome the inertia of tradition?

- How might we incorporate systems thinking to measure the gap, and make it visible?

PRACTICING CREATIVE LEADERSHIP

Of course, if we want to move closer to vision with our team, we will have to move beyond the theoretical model and put creative leadership into practice. Here are some simple ways to implement creative leadership:

Leading the committee

You have been asked to chair a committee or a working group. Where should you start? Begin by strengthening the imagination and core beliefs of the committee members. Look for simple ways to engage their imagination. Take steps to encourage new mindsets that will create a culture of growth, experimentation, and collaboration. As you work, clarify the committee's purpose and define a clear vision of what you want to create.

Working together, create a visual map of the committee's journey, the next steps, and where you see them in that progression. Expect them to bring ideas. When they do, make sure to honor their contributions, and don't be afraid to depart from tradition. When things get challenging, acknowledge the pain and identify it as one of the components of the creative process. When the committee is making good progress – call out the momentum you are feeling.

Facilitating a discussion

So much of how we process the world around us is through our visual senses, but so much of our meetings and discussions rely solely on the words that are spoken. The next time you have an opportunity to facilitate a discussion, change the focus and energy in the room by bringing in a canvas. The canvas could be a large whiteboard, TV monitor, or posterboard. Even just writing words on the canvas will help group members retain critical ideas in the conversation. Adding symbols, pictures, and visual metaphors will help to engage the group. If you are trying to determine the best route to take, draw each route or option on the canvas. Give them a clever name to help members hold them in their memory as you note next steps, pros/cons, or specific characteristics about each option.

Serving on the board

Let's say that you are serving on the board, but not in a leadership position. Can you still practice creative leadership? Absolutely! You can bring a lot to the table by asking the right questions. You can ask questions to help you see and understand systems and structures. Ask questions about current reality and why it is the way it is. If you are bold, you could ask questions to challenge the status quo.

When you get the chance to speak or contribute, use a visual metaphor to make your point. Draw a picture to help clarify the vision of the organization. But do it from the standpoint of making sure you understand. Keep asking questions until you clearly understand (or until the group has clearly defined) the vision.

Setting group Vision

Working to establish a group's vision is one of the most important things you can do as a creative leader. This is because a clear picture of a desired result sets up a tension resolution system that will motivate and inspire the team to act. The vision should directly address the group's problem or purpose. Write the problem in the form of a challenge question, *"How might we...?"*

To clarify your vision, start with a period of divergence. Name, describe, and discuss all the possible ways that you could solve the problem or accomplish your purpose. Stay with divergence even if it gets quiet and uncomfortable. This is where you have to dig deep for good ideas, because all the easy ideas have been put forward. Sit with that for a while. Lean into it.

Then start to converge. Evaluate each idea (or groups of ideas) and consider which ones might work. Be careful not to gravitate too quickly toward one idea – especially toward the ones that seem easy. Easy is not always best, but the ideas should be feasible. Once you converge around a particular idea or concept, refine it into a vision by crafting a vision statement or making a vision board. Remember, the goal is not to be pithy, catchy, or too succinct – you need clarity. You might need multiple paragraphs and images to clearly describe the vision.

EXERCISE:

Having read through these examples, you can solidify your understanding of the framework by annotating the various elements of creative leadership as they occur in the examples. For instance, use a red pen to underline things that relate to strategies like design thinking. Highlight imaginative fundamental concepts in yellow. Circle ideas that relate to expansive actions such as "develop vision."

Closing the Gap

We have explored fundamental ways to expand the imagination, develop vision, and integrate new mindsets. You now have a new understanding of the framework, vocabulary, and benefits of creative leadership. With this foundation you can work to strengthen your imagination and choose creativity as your approach to leadership. More importantly, you can choose to work with and develop others – embracing their imagination, celebrating their creativity, and helping them achieve their vision.

You shouldn't have any doubt about your inherent creative potential – but if you still look around and compare yourself to others, remember that this approach to leadership is not about flashy, surface-level *style* – it is all about identifying and pursuing a vision.

As we investigated the creative process, how to manifest our imagination, and the principles of design, we have discovered methods to embrace ambiguity and implement visual thinking. Your new ability to identify and leverage the components of the creative process will be very useful as you navigate the complex process of moving groups closer to their destination.

Delving into the expansive actions of creative leadership, we described the power of creative tension, effective teaching, and a culture of innovation to lead others toward closing the gap. Now you know how to develop vision, encourage innovation, and lead group members over the springboard of tradition.

In summary, creative leadership is developing the imaginative and constructive abilities (in ourselves and others) to guide groups as they translate a collective vision into reality. It is a comprehensive approach to leadership that synthesizes creative beliefs, thoughts, and actions into strategies that will help your group move through the creative process.

Now is the time to synthesize these mindsets into your daily actions. It's time to become a creative leader, who will go on to shape the leaders of the future. You already have what it takes! Consider your core beliefs, change your mindset, and embrace your creative potential – *then lead with your imagination.*

I invite you to manifest creative synthesis as you influence, develop, organize, and help your group translate vision into reality. If you are not already leading with synthesis-level creativity – you can start now! Fire up your imagination. Bring it into your program, your research, and your leadership. There is not a wrong way to do it. Push the boundaries of what is possible. Reach for innovation and lead others to do the same. Develop your vision and then close the gap!